Strong Feelings

The Jean Nicod Lectures
François Recanati, editor

The Elm and the Expert: Mentalese and Its Semantics, Jerry A. Fodor (1994)

Naturalizing the Mind, Fred Dretske (1995)

Strong Feelings: Emotion, Addiction, and Human Behavior, Jon Elster (1999)

The 1997 Jean Nicod
Lectures

Strong Feelings
Emotion, Addiction, and
Human Behavior

Jon Elster

A Bradford Book
The MIT Press
Cambridge, Massachusetts
London, England

138411

CNRS Editions will distribute the English-language edition in France, Belgium, and Switzerland.

This book was set in Palatino on Miles 33 by Crane Composition, Inc., and was printed and bound in the United States of America.

First printing, 1999

Library of Congress Cataloging-in-Publication Data
Elster, Jon, 1940–
Strong feelings : emotion, addiction, and human behavior / Jon Elster.
     p.   cm. — (The Jean Nicod lectures ; 1997)
  "A Bradford book."
  Includes bibliographical references and index.
  ISBN 0-262-05056-0 (hardcover : alk. paper)
  1. Emotions. 2. Addicts—Psychology. 3. Compulsive behavior—Etiology. 4.   Substance   abuse—Etiology. 5.   Choice   (Psychology).
I. Title. II. Series.
BF531.475   1999
616.86—dc21

98-26803
CIP

For George and George

Contents

    4.1 The Concept of Culture   85
    4.2 Culture and Emotion   98
    4.3 Culture and Addiction   114

5 Choice, Emotion, and Addiction   135
    5.1 The Concept of Choice   135
    5.2 Choice and Emotion   149
    5.3 Choice and Addiction   165

6 Conclusion   193

    Notes   207
    References   229
    Index   247

Series Foreword

The Jean Nicod Lectures are delivered annually in Paris by a leading philosopher of mind or philosophically oriented cognitive scientist. The 1993 inaugural lectures marked the centenary of the birth of the French philosopher and logician Jean Nicod (1893–1931). The lectures are sponsored by the Centre National de la Recherche Scientifique (CNRS) and are organized in cooperation with the Fondation Maison des Sciences de l'Homme (MSH Foundation). The series hosts the texts of the lectures or the monographs they inspire.

Jacques Bouveresse, President of the Jean Nicod Committee

Jean-Gabriel Ganascia, Director of the Cognitive Science Program (GIS Sciences de la Cognition)

François Recanati, Secretary of the Jean Nicod Committee and Editor of the Series

Jean Nicod Committee

Mario Borillo

Jean-Pierre Changeux

André Holley
Michel Imbert
Pierre Jacob
Jacques Mehler
Elisabeth Pacherie
Philippe de Rouilhan
Dan Sperber

Preface and Acknowledgments

The present book is a revised and expanded version of the Jean Nicod Lectures that I gave in Paris in June 1997. It draws on two main sources. The first is work on the emotions that I began in 1985 and continued through the 1990s, resulting in the publication of *Alchemies of the Mind* in 1998. The discussion of emotions in chapter 2 and sections 4.2 and 5.2 below draws extensively on that treatment, while also refocusing it for the specific aims I pursue here. The second is work on addiction that I began in 1992. Although I have already published some articles on this topic, chapter 3 and sections 4.3 and 5.3 below provide a fuller and more general discussion.

For the idea of treating emotions and addiction as cases of "strong feelings" I am indebted to George Loewenstein's research program on "visceral factors" in behavior. The book also owes much to our collaboration in the Working Group on Intertemporal Choice, supported by the Russell Sage Foundation. My thinking about addiction, and about choice more generally, is greatly inspired by the path-breaking work of George Ainslie and by many discussions with him over the years. This book is dedicated, therefore, to George and George.

My thinking about addiction has also developed through discussions in a working group on addiction consisting of George Ainslie, Eliot Gardner, Olav Gjelsvik, Aanund Hylland, George Loewenstein, Karl Ove Moene, Jørg Mørland, Thomas Schelling, Ole-Jørgen Skog, and Helge Waal. The work of the group has been funded by the Norwegian Research Council, the Norwegian Institute for Alcohol and Drug Research, the Norwegian Directorate for the Prevention of Alcohol and Drug Problems, and the Russell Sage Foundation.

I received written comments on an earlier version of chapter 3 from George Ainslie, James Fearon, Avram Goldstein, Olav Gjelsvik, David Laibson, Jørg Mørland, Wiktor Osiatynski, and Ole-Jørgen Skog. Finally, I want to thank my research assistant, Joshua Rosenstein, as well as Cheryl Seleski and the marvelously efficient library staff at the Russell Sage Foundation, which provided me with a fellowship to finish this book.

Strong Feelings

1   Introduction

In this study of emotion and addiction I set myself a methodological task and a theoretical one. On the one hand, I shall explore the relation between causal and conceptual analysis in the study of human behavior. What is the relation between the *definition* of emotion or addiction and the *explanation* of the same phenomenon? That is, to what extent do the emotions or the addictions form *natural kinds*? On the other hand, I shall discuss the relation between three explanatory approaches to behavior: neurobiology, culture, and choice, including the special case of rational choice. Intuitively, it seems clear that because of their peculiar physiological strength, emotions and addictive cravings can short-circuit choice or at least distort the rationality of choice. Yet like all preanalytical intuitions, this one needs to be carefully scrutinized. I also ask to what extent emotions and cravings are physiologically hardwired and to what extent they are cultural constructions.

Emotions and the various states induced by addictive substances are special cases of what George Loewen-stein has called *visceral factors* in behavior.[1] This more general category also includes drives such as hunger, thirst, and sexual desire; urges to urinate, defecate, or sleep; as well as organic disturbances such as pain, fatigue, vertigo, and nausea. In their extreme forms, these states go together with strong physiological changes that can interfere with the capacity for making choices, or at least rational choices. Negotiators, for instance, are advised to abstain from drinking coffee because its diuretic effects distract attention from the matter at hand. At the same time, they may crave coffee to resist drowsiness.

These visceral states differ from emotions and addiction-related states in that they are less closely linked to cognition and culture. By and large, emotions are triggered by beliefs. Addictive cravings too can be triggered by the belief that a drug is available and be extinguished by the belief that it is unavailable. Also, emotions and cravings are powerfully shaped by the fact that they are culturally defined *as* emotions and cravings. By contrast, the acute thirst of the person who has been in the desert for a long time without water, the need to urinate of a person who has gone for a long time without doing so, and the overwhelming drowsiness of a person who has gone without sleep for several days are essentially independent of cognition and culture.

More generally, we may distinguish three ways in which cognition may be involved in these visceral factors. First, a visceral state may be triggered by a belief. Second, once triggered, a visceral motivation can be further shaped by the belief that it is that particular kind of motivation. To illustrate, a person may feel envy at the sight of a more successful friend and then shame once he recognizes that he is feeling envious. A heavy drinker may change his self-image and his behavior once he begins to believe that he is an alcoholic. Third, the motivation may have an intentional object: it may be *about* something. Some visceral factors, such as pain or vertigo, have none of these cognitive aspects. Others, such as thirst and sexual desire, have intentional objects but are not triggered or shaped by beliefs. Cravings have intentional objects (they are cravings *for* drugs). They are also susceptible of being triggered and shaped by beliefs, although to a lesser degree than emotions. Emotions stand out among the visceral motivations because they typically, or at least frequently, involve cognition in all three ways.

These are rough characterizations, which allow for nuances and exceptions. People are often turned on sexually by the belief that their partner is turned on. A driver may be aware that he is about to fall asleep and fight against his drowsiness. Emotions such as fear can be triggered by perceptions as well as by cognitions. Yet I believe that in standard cases these various motivational factors can be uncontroversially located on a continuum. At one extreme we have the noncognitive or purely visceral states of pain, drowsiness, etc. Next are the states that have intentional objects but are not otherwise shaped by cognition, such as hunger, thirst, and sexual desire. Further, there are cravings that have intentional objects and that can also involve cognitions in other ways. Then there are emotions, which often involve cognition in all three ways. At the other extreme of the continuum, there are motivational states that do not imply any arousal or viscerality at all, as in my calm decision to take an umbrella because I believe it will rain and I don't want to get wet.

The states at either extreme of the continuum have opposite implications for choice. Although the behaviors induced by drowsiness, fatigue, and pain are more complicated than simple reflex actions, they often have a similar involuntary quality. A car driver may fight off drowsiness and a mountain climber resist muscle fatigue, but not indefinitely. To fall asleep or to lose one's grip on the rope is not to *do* anything: it's merely an event, something that happens. At the other extreme, rational decision making undisturbed by arousal is the paradigm of free, voluntary choice. In between these extremes are the cases that interest me here, those in which behavior is affected by arousal as well as by choice. Among these cases, I exclude the physiological drives from my concern, mainly because they are culturally invariant. I study emotion and addiction because they allow me to examine the triangular contrast of *neurobiology, culture,* and *choice,* rather than any simple dichotomy.

Before I proceed, I should clarify two points that should be obvious but may not be. First, when I contrast neurobiology with culture and choice, I do not imply that the latter phenomena have no neurobiological substrate. I take it for granted that *all* human behavior and all mental states have a neurobiological foundation; in fact, the denial of this view is not so much false as incomprehensible. I use "neurobiology" simply as a shorthand for the neural mechanisms that generate the arousal as well as the euphoria or dysphoria that characterize most emotions and cravings. Although beliefs too must rely on similar mechanisms, we know so little about the neurobiology of the complex beliefs that enter into cravings and emotions that it would be pointless to insist on their underlying substrate.

To illustrate, let me draw on a suggestion by Michael Liebowitz that "the chemistry of love" is like that of the amphetamines.[2] We know a great deal about the neurophysiology of amphetamines and how they produce the characteristic effects of acute awareness, heightened energy, reduced need for sleep and food, feelings of euphoria, etc. These effects run a predictable course, lasting for several hours and then turning into depression. The symptoms are strikingly similar to those of love, in the sense of acute infatuation, or what Dorothy Tennov calls "limerence,"[3] and it is entirely possible that love and amphetamines recruit some of the same neural circuits. Yet there is also a striking difference. The high from an amphetamine is produced by the intake of a chemical *substance*. The euphoria of love can be produced by a *belief* that the other person loves oneself and may turn into dysphoria when the belief is disconfirmed.[4] The euphoria and dysphoria can arise virtually instantly, whereas the effects of an amphetamine are produced and wear off more gradually. Whereas the neural pathway by which the chemical substance produces its effects is now being elucidated, the chemistry of the belief that one's love is requited and the effect of that belief on the reward system in the brain are likely to be vastly more complicated. For the foreseeable future, and perhaps forever, we will only be able to describe that belief in terms of its content ("She loves me"), and not in terms of its molecular substrate.

Second, any reference to "culture" is also a shorthand. It is not intended to deny the principle of methodological individualism, the denial of which, once again, is not so much false as incomprehensible. When I say that a culture or a society "induces" specific concepts and beliefs, or that it "condemns" or "approves" certain practices, I mean *only* (i) that individuals in that culture share the concepts, beliefs, values, or norms, and know that they share them, and (ii) that individuals in some other cultures lack the concepts, beliefs, or norms in question. By assumption (ii), the concepts, beliefs, and norms shared by individuals must be due to their upbringing and socialization within a particular society, rather than to universal features of the human condition. Every culture must have the concept of a sunset, but not all cultures have the concept of guilt. In this sense, the *concept* of guilt is "socially constructed." As we shall see in section 4.2, however, this does not imply that the *emotion* of guilt is a social construction.

The book is organized around parallel analyses of emotion and addiction, to bring out similarities as well as differences. In addition to their comparison, we may also consider how emotion and addiction may interact with one another. On the one hand, it has been claimed that one can become *addicted to emotion*. These include claims that it is possible to be addicted to the emotion of hybris or pridefulness, induced by the belief that one is superior to others;[5] also that one can become addicted to love, either to love in general[6] or to love for a specific person.[7] I shall not pursue these suggestions, which seem too speculative or metaphorical to warrant further discussion. On the other hand, there is the more plausible idea, discussed in chapter 4 below, that *emotion can have a causal role in addiction*, because many addicts are prone to feelings of guilt and shame that may perpetuate their addiction or, on the contrary, induce them to break it.

Both emotion and addiction are elusive categories. It is not easy to know which specific feelings or cravings to include under these headings. Is surprise an emotion? Is compulsive gambling an addiction? Given an uncontroversial instance of emotion or addiction, such as fear or alcoholism, one might define a given phenomenon as emotional or addictive if it is analogous in some respects to these core cases. But since everything is a little bit like everything else, analogy is a weak tool for analysis.[8]

For scientific purposes, homology is a much more powerful instrument than analogy. On the basis of analogy, it is tempting to classify whales and sharks together as one group (animals that live in water) and birds and bats as another group (animals that fly). On the basis of homology, that is, a common causal history, whales and bats have much more in common than any other pair among these four animals (figure 1.1). Knowledge of the reproductive system or metabolism of whales enables us to formulate hypotheses for bats, and vice versa. By contrast, animals that are related only by analogy are unlikely to have much more in common than the features that define the analogy *and other features that flow causally from those features.*

The italicized expression points to a useful, if limited, role of analogy in scientific reasoning. If we want to explore the metabolism of sharks, there is no reason to privilege hypotheses derived from the metabolism of whales. If, however, we want to examine the hydrodynamic properties of one animal that lives in water, knowing the features of other aquatic animals is probably going to be useful. Even more obviously, if we want to understand how bats manage to stay in the air, know-

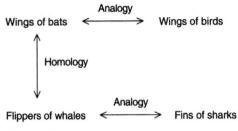

Figure 1.1
Homology is a much more powerful instrument than analogy.

ing how birds do it is likely to be of help. In his classic study *On Growth and Form*, D'Arcy Wentworth Thompson writes, for instance, "We know ... how in strict accord with theory ... the wing, whether of bird or insect, stands stiff along its 'leading edge,' like the mast before the sail; and how, conversely, it thins out exquisitely fine along its rear or 'trailing edge,' where sharp discontinuity favours the formation of uplifting eddies."[9]

The features underlying a homology owe their existence to a *common causal history*. The features underlying an analogy may have entirely different causal histories but nevertheless generate *similar causal effects*. I shall refer to the features that define an analogy as *primary features*, and to those that are causally implicated by the primary ones as *secondary features*. Thus the primary feature of the analogy between birds and bats is that they can maintain themselves in the air without relying on an initial impetus, being in that respect similar to airplanes but different from both flying fish and rockets. The secondary features are those that follow from the aerodynamic constraints on any heavy body that is to maintain itself in the air.

Let me anticipate chapter 3 and use some examples from addiction to show the relevance of these concepts to the problem at hand. Students of addiction now agree that most chemical addictions are homologous, in the sense that their euphoric and dysphoric effects derive from very similar (but not identical) mechanisms in the dopaminergic reward systems of the brain. By contrast, chemical addictions and behavioral phenomena such as compulsive gambling or overeating may be no more than analogous, in the sense, say, of being characterized by strong urges to engage in activities with harmful long-term consequences. These urges constitute the primary features of these analogous phenomena. If the urge to drink and the urge to gamble rely on entirely different neural mechanisms, we cannot rely on one of these putative addictions to make predictions about the extent of withdrawal, tolerance, or sensitization that will be observed in the other. Yet if the urge induces self-destructive behavior, we can predict that it will come to be resisted. We can predict, moreover, that regardless of the origin of the urge, its coexistence with a strong desire to resist it will generate shame, denial, rationalization, the development of self-control strategies, and other phenomena with clear behavioral implications. These consequences are secondary features of many addictions.

These secondary features arise because human addicts are capable of being aware of their addiction, deploring it, and trying to overcome it. The animals used in experimental studies of addiction, notably rats and monkeys, do not have these cognitive and moral capacities. Because the neurophysiology of chemical addiction is essentially the same in humans and other animals ("animals" for short), many of the behavioral patterns are quite similar, especially in the earlier stages of addiction. Cravings for cocaine, for instance, will induce similar extreme drug-seeking behavior in rats and humans.[10] Yet in later stages of addiction, when the long-term adverse consequences begin to appear, human addicts display quite different responses. It is often said, I believe correctly, that ambivalence is the hallmark of addiction in humans. Animals, by contrast, rarely show behavioral signs of ambivalence.[11]

A similar contrast between human and animal behavior exists in the case of the emotions. Animals are incapable of holding the kind of complex beliefs that enter into many human emotions. In particular, they are incapable (as far as we know) of holding beliefs about their own emotions. Whereas the behavioral expressions of the human emotions of anger, fear, or love can be strongly modulated by the agent's aware-ness of them, in animals the link between emotion and behavior is not mediated by cognition. Human beings can feel shame at being afraid, for instance, and try to hide their fear or present it as mere prudence. To my knowledge, no animals are capable of being ashamed of their fear.

We see, therefore, how cognition, including moral beliefs, plays a dual role in the study of emotion and addiction. On the one hand, it serves to differentiate the specifically human forms of these phenomena from those observed in animals. On the other hand, it helps us to understand why emotion and addiction may take different forms in different cultures, depending on their specific cognitive and moral tenets. Because of the importance of cognition, one must go beyond animal studies to study the behavioral expressions of emotion and addiction. Because cognition varies across cultures, one cannot assume that these expressions in humans are universal and hardwired. Nor, however, should one assume that the expressions are endlessly malleable. Although culture may modulate and shape emotions and cravings, that very statement presupposes that there exist precultural or transcultural tendencies to be modified and shaped in the first place.

The strategy of the rest of the book is as follows. Chapters 2 and 3 study emotion and addiction according to a common scheme, which progresses from empirical survey through phenomenological description to causal analysis. First, I enumerate a number of feelings and cravings that are frequently subsumed under the headings of emotion and addiction. This step in the procedure is entirely preanalytical and serves only to give a rough idea of the range of phenomena to be discussed. Next, for each of the two classes of phenomena, I enumerate a number of observable features often used to characterize or define them. This step is conceptual or phenomenological. Ideally, it would offer necessary and sufficient conditions for something to be an emotion or an addiction. Third, I try to summarize our knowledge about the causal mechanisms that generate emotions and addictive cravings. Once we have identified these mechanisms, we may go back and revise the set of phenomenological features that characterize emotions and addiction, as well as the set of behaviors that fall under these headings. Thus phenomena that seem analogous at the phenomenological level may turn out to lack homology at the causal level, or vice versa. Until we understand the causal mechanisms of emotion and addiction, we cannot know what emotions and addictions are, nor can we know what emotions and addictions there are. It turns out that we know much more about the neurophysiology of addiction than we do about emotion. On the basis of what is known about the causal mechanisms involved, it seems safe to say that the chemical addictions do form a natural kind. Whether the emotions do remains an unresolved issue.

In chapters 4 and 5, I focus on *culture* and *choice* as determinants of emotional and addictive behavior. As noted earlier, culture is a specifically human phenomenon—a fact that helps us both to distinguish between animal and human behavior and to compare the varieties of emotion and addiction in different societies. Choice, by contrast, is not a uniquely human phenomenon. Animals too are capable of weighing alternatives against one another and choosing between them on the basis of their consequences or rewards. Yet the fact that only humans are capable of making *rational* choices has important implications for emotions and addictive cravings. Even for humans, however, we can ask whether emotions and cravings might sometimes be so strong as to short-circuit rational choice, or even choice altogether. At their strongest, these urges seem to have an overpowering quality that leaves little room for comparison and choice.

2   Emotion

2.1   How Do We Know What We Know about Emotion?

Let us begin with introspection. All nonpathological individuals have felt anger and shame, to name but two of the emotions, and most of us have experienced many other emotions as well. Introspective knowledge is both indispensable and insufficient. It would be difficult to understand why shame can be so overwhelmingly powerful as to drive people to suicide if we had not ourselves been in the grip of this emotion. A person who had never known shame might be tempted to explain a suicide by the material sanctions that are imposed on an ostracized person rather than by the subjective feeling of pain and unworthiness that is induced by the sanctions.

At the same time, introspection is not enough. For one thing, some individuals might never have experienced a particular emotion. Montaigne, for instance, says, "About envy I can say virtually nothing: that passion which is portrayed as so powerful and violent has no hold on me."[1] The manifest inadequacy of Hume's treatment of the same emotion may also be due to lack of personal acquaintance with it.[2] For another, the emotion might be so strong as to blot out cognitive analysis. Again I can cite Montaigne, who cites Petrarch to the effect that "He who can describe how his heart is ablaze is burning on a small pyre."[3] We cannot observe our anger when we are in its grip, and there is no guarantee that our later memory serves us well either. In fact, very traumatic experiences may not leave any memory trace at all.

To some extent we can overcome the limitations of introspection by supplementing it with observation of other people under everyday, noncontrolled circumstances. This source of insight also has its limitations, of course. For reasons that may or may not have to do with their own emotional makeup, some people are inept at interpreting the emotions of others. They make mistakes of underinterpretation as well as of overinterpretation, as when they ignore expressions of hostility in others or find signs of nonexistent affection. Yet some people seem to have unerring skill and insight in interpreting what others do and say in terms of their underlying emotions. Some novelists and playwrights, in particular, display a superb understanding of the human emotions. Although I have learned most from Jane Austen and Stendhal, many others could be cited.[4] The writings of the moralists, from Seneca and Plutarch to Montaigne and La Rochefoucauld, are another almost inexhaustible source of insights. At a more systematic level, a handful of philosophers, from Aristotle to Hume, have been able to distill from their experience some general propositions about the emotions. When all is said and done, these writers—playwrights and novelists, moralists and philosophers—remain the most important sources for the study of human emotions.

Yet this is not to say that more scientific sources have nothing to contribute. A great deal of what we know about the emotions draws on history, social science, and natural science. The relevant contributions fall in two categories. On the one hand, historical and anthropological studies can enhance our knowledge of the varieties of emotional behavior. On the other hand, psychological, biological, and neuroscientific studies aim at discovering the fine grain of emotional mechanisms. Let me comment on each category of writings in turn.

If emotions were universal—if the same emotions were found everywhere to the same extent and triggered by the same situations—there would be no need to go beyond the modern Western societies that I (and most readers of this book) know best. Yet, as I argue in section 4.2 below, emotions are not universal *in this sense*. (They may or may not be universal in another sense, also considered in section 4.2.) From historical and anthropological studies we can learn that there is a great deal of variation in the range of emotions expressed and in the situations that elicit them. Even when these studies do not directly address the issue of the emotions, they can offer evidence of behavior that can be interpreted in terms of specific emotions and can illuminate those emotions in return. An example of what I have in mind is an outstanding study of feuding in nineteenth-century Corsica by Stephen Wilson. Being exclusively based on legal and administrative documents, the book does not contain any explicit state-

ments about the emotional states of the various participants in the feud. Yet by their cumulative weight the
facts that Wilson adduces allow us to form a view of
the various emotions—anger, fear, hatred, envy—
involved in the feud. He writes, for instance, that in 1845
one "Antono Santalucia . . . shot Antono Quilichini, the
sixth of the witnesses against his brother in the 1840
trial to be killed," and that on another occasion "a
notary from Novale was convicted of homicide on false
testimony and subsequently died in prison. His brother
became a bandit and over a period of years killed all 14
prosecution witnesses."[5] These are extremes of vindictiveness that we do not know from our own societies.
They tell us that the emotion in question is not garden-
variety anger, which, as Aristotle noted, tends to spend
itself quickly.[6]

For the basic causal mechanisms involved in emotion—how emotions are triggered and how they may
trigger behavior—we must look to psychology and the
various biological sciences. The relevant studies fall in
four main categories. First, there is the experimental
study of normal human subjects. This is the paradigm
of most psychological research on the emotions. Typically, emotions serve as explananda rather than expla-
nantia: the dependent variable tends to be an emotion
rather than another mental state or a behavior to be
explained in terms of emotion. Also, the emotion is typically measured through self-reports rather than
through any of the observable features associated with
it (see below). The usual paradigm is to ask subjects to
report what emotions they have felt or would feel in
various situations, in order to correlate different emotions with different situational antecedents. In some

studies, however, the dependent variable is behavioral. In experiments with the "Ultimatum Game," for instance, subjects are given the opportunity of hurting another subject to retaliate for unfair treatment, even if the retaliation hurts them as well.[7] The general finding is that if the treatment is sufficiently unfair, subjects do indeed take the opportunity to get even. Although the experiments are usually not designed with a view to decide which emotion is involved—envy, anger, or indignation—it should be possible to do so.[8]

Many of these studies are subject to methodological problems that affect their usefulness. Self-reports are notoriously fragile. Even when the results of self-report studies are reliable (i.e., replicable), they may not be valid (i.e., they may not measure that they are supposed to measure). Studies that induce behavior through rewards or withholding of rewards may suffer from the problem that the sums involved are so small that the subjects behave differently from what they would do in real-life situations with higher stakes, either because they do not pay much attention or because they want to please the experimenter. Yet this problem may not be as acute as is often assumed. By using first-world research grants to study third-world subjects, Cameron has been able to show that subjects in the ultimatum game behave in the same ("irrational" or "emotional") way when the stakes are high enough to matter.[9] The self-report problem is more serious, among other reasons, because of a systematic tendency to underestimate the subjective impact of past, future, or hypothetical visceral feelings.[10]

Second, there is the study of human patients with brain lesions that induce cognitive, emotional, or behavioral pathologies. In *Descartes' Error*, Antonio Damasio draws on work with these patients to argue against the age-old view that emotions are an obstacle to rational decision making. On his theory, emotions emerge instead as an essential precondition for rationality. In patients with prefrontal damage he observed both a certain emotional flatness and a tendency to procrastinate over the most trivial decisions. He concludes that we owe our ability to make speedy decisions when time is of the essence to our reliance on "somatic markers" or, in the vernacular, "gut feelings." I return to his ideas in chapter 5 below.

Third, there is the experimental study of animal behavior, mainly in rats and monkeys. Here the experimenter can not only manipulate environmental variables but also use surgical interventions to modify the physiology of the animal. By destroying some organs while preserving others, one can determine the specific physiological pathways involved in some of the main emotional reactions. The best-studied emotion is probably that of *fear*, which has been the object of pathbreaking work by Joseph LeDoux, summarized in *The Emotional Brain*.[11] I return to his findings and conjectures in sections 2.2 and 2.3 below, and then again in chapter 4. For the time being, let me only note that the relevance of experimental studies of animals for the study of human emotions is severely limited. Many, perhaps most, human emotions are elicited by beliefs of a complexity beyond what animals are thought to be capable of.

Fourth, there is the observation of animals in the wild or under seminatural conditions, such as a zoo. Many will have seen the TV programs by Jane Goodall featuring the chimpanzee Frodo, who is shown first as consumed with envy when his younger brother replaces him in the affections of his mother, then as dancing with joy when the brother dies, and finally dying of grief after his mother dies. Although I have no competence to judge the validity of this particular presentation, it seems plausible that studies of animals in their natural habitat can offer useful information about their emotional lives. De Waal has demonstrated, for instance, guilt (or shame?) in subordinate macaques by giving them access to females and allowing them to copulate in the absence of the alpha male and then watching their more-than-usually submissive behavior when he returned.[12] Yet in many cases it is not clear whether the relevant cognitive antecedents obtain. In animals other than humans, it may be difficult to decide whether what looks like an emotional reaction is triggered by a mental representation of the situation or is merely a learned response. The apparent guilt of a dog that has shredded newspapers in its owner's absence may simply be a conditioned fear of punishment, since the same response is produced when the owner himself shreds the newspapers and leaves them on the floor.[13]

To summarize, let me distinguish the emotions along two dimensions: strong versus weak, and having complex versus simple cognitive antecedents. In societies that have passed beyond the constant struggle for survival, the most important emotions are characterized by high arousal and valence (see below) and by complex cognitive antecedents. Examples include anger produced by a belief that a rival has used immoral means to obtain a promotion one covets and joy produced by a belief that the person one loves reciprocates the feeling. For technical, financial, and ethical reasons, strong emotions cannot be produced in laboratory experiments on human beings. For reasons of developmental complexity, emotions with complex cognitive antecedents cannot be produced in animals other than humans. Because of these limitations, I feel justified in asserting that most of what we know about strong and complex emotions is based on literature and philosophy rather than on scientific studies. As will become clear, I do not by any means exclude controlled studies or systematic observations as sources of knowledge about the emotions, yet if we want to understand the emotions as *the stuff of life*—what keeps us awake at night and makes us hope beyond hope—they take second place.

2.2   What Emotions There Are

Before trying to address this issue, it might seem necessary to specify the context: what emotions are there in society x or in culture y? I postpone this issue until chapter 4. Here I shall naively limit myself to the emotions that can be identified in modern Western societies. Whether they also exist elsewhere, or everywhere, and whether other cultures display emotions not found in ours are issues that I leave aside for the time being.

Although language can serve as a useful first approximation to the enumeration and classification of emotions, it cannot be the final authority. In the first place, language cannot tell us whether words such as "surprise" or "frustration" are emotion terms or not. In the second place, language cannot tell us when two emotion terms—"fury" and "rage," or "guilt" and "re-

morse"—are synonyms and when they denote different emotions. In the third place, language may have
gaps. Although we differentiate among grief, regret,
and disappointment, there is only a single term,
"relief," for the corresponding positive emotions.
Although Descartes used "indignation" to refer to *A*'s
emotion when he sees *B* slighting *C*,[14] ordinary language does not restrict the word to this special case, for
which no separate term exists. To resolve such issues,
we need a more theoretical characterization of the emotions. I discuss this issue in the following sections. For
now I shall only offer a preanalytical survey of what
seems uncontroversially to count as emotions, together
with some comments on borderline cases. I shall characterize these emotions as positive or negative, depending on whether they are experienced as pleasurable or painful.

An important group of emotions are what we may
call the *social emotions*. They involve a positive or a negative evaluation of one's own or someone else's behavior
or character. These three dichotomies yield eight emotions altogether:

• *Shame*: a negative emotion triggered by a belief about
one's own character

• *Contempt* and *hatred*: negative emotions triggered by
beliefs about another's character. (Contempt is induced
by the thought that another is inferior; hatred by the
thought that he is evil.)

• *Guilt*: a negative emotion triggered by a belief about
one's own action

• *Anger*: a negative emotion triggered by a belief about
another's action

• *Pridefulness*: a positive emotion triggered by a belief about one's own character
• *Liking*: a positive emotion triggered by a belief about another's character
• *Pride*: a positive emotion triggered by a belief about one's own action
• *Admiration*: a positive emotion triggered by a belief about another's action

Second, there is a set of emotions generated by the thought that someone else deservedly or undeservedly possesses some good or bad.[15] Following Aristotle's discussion in the *Rhetoric*, we may distinguish six cases:

• *Envy*: a negative emotion caused by the deserved good of someone else
• *Indignation*: a negative emotion caused by the undeserved good of someone else
• *Sympathy*: a positive emotion caused by the deserved good of someone else
• *Pity*: a negative emotion caused by the undeserved misfortune of someone else
• *Malice*: a positive emotion caused by the undeserved misfortune of someone else
• *Gloating*: a positive emotion caused by the deserved misfortune of someone else

Third, there are positive or negative emotions generated by the thought of good or bad things that have happened or will happen to oneself—joy and grief, with their several varieties and cognates. As many have observed, bad events in the past may also generate positive emotions in the present, and good events negative emotions.[16] Thus in the main collection of proverbial sayings from antiquity, the *Sentences* of Publilius Syrus, we find both "The remembrance of past perils is pleasant" and "Past happiness augments present misery."

All the emotions discussed so far are induced by beliefs that are held in the mode of certainty. More accurately, they are capable of being induced by beliefs held in that mode, although some of them may also occur with less-than-certain beliefs. There are also emotions—hope, fear, love, and jealousy—that essentially involve beliefs held in the modes of probability or possibility. These emotions are generated by the thought of good or bad things that may or may not happen in the future and of good or bad states of affairs that may or may not obtain in the present. By and large, these emotions require that the event or state in question is seen as more than merely conceivable, that is, there must be a nonnegligible chance that it actually occurs or obtains. The thought of winning the big prize in the lottery may generate hope, but not that of receiving a large gift from an unknown millionaire. These emotions also seem to require that the event or state fall short of being thought to be certain. If I *know* that am about to be executed, I will feel grief or despair rather than fear. According to Stendhal and Tennov, love withers away both when one is certain that it is reciprocated and when one is certain that it is not. According to La Rochefoucauld and Proust, jealousy may disappear the moment one *knows* that the person one loves is in love with somebody else.[17]

There are also emotions generated by *counterfactual* thoughts about what might have happened or what might have been done. These include negative emo-

tions of regret and disappointment, together with the
corresponding positive emotions that I subsumed
under the heading of relief. These are not moral emotions. In the case of disappointment, there was nothing
one could have done; in the case of regret, there is nothing one could and should have done. Although some
people blame themselves for bad outcomes that they
could have prevented even when they could not have
known what to do at the time ("If I had only called him
up, he would have left later and not been killed in the
accident"), these are cases of (irrational) guilt, not
regret.

A related class of emotions are the wistful or ominous
feelings triggered by *subjunctive* beliefs about events
that might conceivably happen, although not with sufficient probability to generate hope or fear. Many day-
dreams fall in this category. A seemingly related but
subtly different set of emotions are those induced by
works of art that tell some kind of story: novels, plays,
and films. Although the issue is difficult and controversial,[18] I believe that the emotion I experience when reading about an experience that would have caused me to
feel joy had it happened to me *is* joy. From introspection, it seems that the emotion I feel when a character
in a TV play is making a fool of himself in public is very
similar or even identical to the vicarious shame I feel
when a friend is doing the same in a real-life situation.
I cringe and want to stop watching or to leave. Emotions
may also be induced by works of art that do not rest on
any narrative; music, in particular, has the capacity to
induce purified emotions of joy, grief, triumph, and the
like. Yet with one exception, there do not seem to be
any emotions induced by works of art that we do not

also experience outside the world of art. The exception is the aesthetic emotions—wonder, awe, and the like—that are induced by purely formal structures of works of art.

Above I have listed some twenty-odd mental states which I have claimed are emotions. In some cases, the claim can hardly be contested. If love, anger, or fear are not emotions, what is? In other cases, there is room for disagreement. Some might claim that regret is not an emotion, only a wish that one had acted differently. Others might argue that hope need not be an emotion, only a belief that something may be the case and a desire that it be the case. And still others might think that what I have called aesthetic emotions is in fact purely intellectual appreciation. Other borderline or controversial cases include surprise, boredom, interest, sexual desire, enjoyment, worry, and frustration. I shall now move from discussing what emotions there are to considering what emotions are, to see if that will help us resolve these disagreements.

2.3 What Emotions Are: Phenomenological Analysis

The emotions can be characterized by a number of features that are immediately observable, prior to any scientific analysis. Although we shall see that none of them are necessary features of all states that intuitively or preanalytically qualify as emotions, each plays an important part in emotional life. To make a simple analogy, it is not true that all furniture is heavy. Paper lanterns are furniture, and yet they weigh almost nothing. Yet for many practical purposes, heaviness is an important property of furniture. Similarly, the fact that some emotions are triggered by perception rather than by cognition does not undermine the importance of cognition as an antecedent of emotion. Hence in this section I will take the question "What are emotions?" in the sense of "What are the characteristic properties of emotions?" rather than "What are necessary and sufficient properties for a mental state to be an emotion?"

First, however, I need to make a long-overdue distinction. The word "emotion" can be taken either in an occurrent or in a dispositional sense. Occurrent emotions are actual episodes of experiencing anger, fear, joy, and the like. Emotional dispositions are propensities to have occurrent emotions, such as irascibility, faintheartedness, or what we call a "sunny disposition." Prejudices such as misogyny or anti-Semitism are also emotional dispositions. The disposition might be characterized in terms of the threshold for triggering the emotion (e.g., irritability), in terms of the strength of the emotion when triggered (e.g., irascibility), or both. Even irascible people are not angry all the time, and an angry person need not be irascible, so the two phenomena are distinct. Usually, it will be clear from the context whether I am referring to occurrent emotions or to dispositions, but when necessary I shall make it explicit.

Most of the time, most of the occurrent emotions enumerated in section 2.2 have the following properties:[19]

- Unique qualitative "feel"
- Sudden onset
- Unbidden occurrence
- Brief duration
- Triggered by a cognitive state

- Directed toward an intentional object
- Inducing physiological changes ("arousal")
- Having physiological and physiognomic expressions
- Inducing specific action tendencies
- Accompanied by pleasure or pain ("valence")

With the possible exception of the first, none of these features seem to be universal properties of what we pretheoretically identify as emotions. Below I shall in fact provide counterexamples for each of them. They cannot, therefore, be used to *define* emotion. One might, perhaps, take a purely pragmatic approach and say that something is an emotion if it possesses (say) six of the ten properties. Yet because there is no practical need to decide whether something is or is not an emotion, this procedure is pointless.

Unique Qualitative "Feel"

Introspectively, each emotion is experienced as having a special feel or *quale*, much as each color is perceived as having a unique qualitative aspect. We must ask, however, whether this feel is anything over and above the subjective perception of the other properties of an occurrent emotion. The best evidence that it is may come from the perception of music. Malcolm Budd argues, for instance, that "when you hear music as being expressive of emotion E—when you hear E in the music—you hear the music sounding like the way E feels."[20] When I hear a sorrowful piece of music, what I experience is pure grief—not very intense grief (because there is no arousal and no action tendency), but unmistakably grief. The case of joy is a bit more complex, since joyful music does tend to induce action and its characteristic expressions. Yet it strains belief to argue that the feeling of joy simply *is* the pleasurable perception of arousal, action tendency, etc. Also, when emotions are induced by direct brain stimulation or by chemical means subjects often describe their experience in terms that suggest the existence of emotional qualia.[21] The question is opaque, however. Since it is at most a marginal one in the study of the emotions, I shall not pursue it further.

Sudden Onset

According to Paul Ekman, "Quick onset is fundamental . . . to the adaptive value of emotions, mobilizing us to respond to important events with little time required for consideration or preparation."[22] I return to the question of adaptation in section 2.4 below. For the time being, I only want to make two remarks. First, it is indeed true that in many standard cases, emotional reactions are triggered almost instantaneously by cognitive or perceptual cues. In the face of physical aggression or danger, the emotions of anger and fear, with the concomitant action tendencies of freezing, fleeing, or fighting, can arise in a split second. Second, however, there are so many exceptions that a sudden onset cannot be taken as a universal characteristic or defining feature of emotion. Anger and love, for instance, may creep up on us so gradually and imperceptibly that we do not notice what is happening. At the same time, these emotions are often characterized by a "point of no return" beyond which self-control is of no avail.[23] The reason that anger is so hard to control, according to Montaigne,

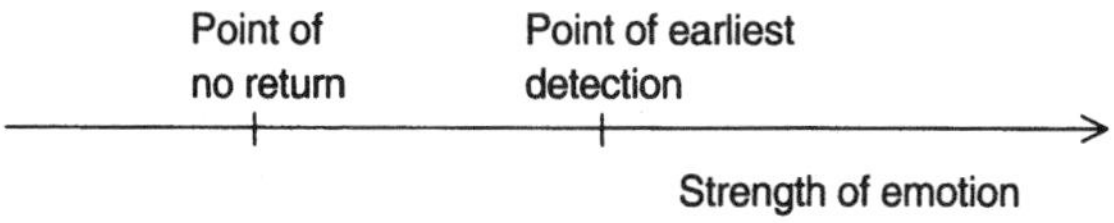

Figure 2.1
The dilemma of the dynamics of love and anger.

is that we lose control before we become aware of the emotion. "The infancies of all things are feeble and weak. We must keep our eyes open at their beginnings; you cannot find the danger then because it is so small; once it has grown, you cannot find the cure."[24] In a seventeenth-century novel *Le Grand Cyrus*, we find a similar observation about love: "Cleobuline loved him without thinking that she loved him, and she was under this illusion for so long that the affection could not be overcome when she finally became aware of it."[25] The dynamics of anger and love, in other words, is subject to the dilemma in figure 2.1.

Unbidden Occurrence

A synonym for "emotion" is "passion," which is closely related to "passive." Although the origin of words can never provide an argument for a substantive conclusion, in this case etymology happens to fit the traditional view that emotions are passively undergone rather than actively chosen. Emotional reactions are *events*, not *actions*. In spite of various recent arguments to the contrary, I believe that the traditional view is roughly correct. I return to the issue at greater length in section 5.2 below. Here, I shall only observe that the property of being involuntary is not a universal or defining characteristic of the emotions. We may, for instance, decide to get angry by thinking about an occurrence that has made us angry in the past, or to work up a grief by exploiting feedback from expressions of the emotion to experience the emotion itself. Yet as these examples suggest, intentionally produced emotions are parasitic on involuntary ones. If certain beliefs did not spontaneously generate a specific emotion, one could not cause it to occur by calling them up, and if certain expressions did not spontaneously accompany a specific emotion, one could not bring it about by simulating them.

Brief Duration

To cite Ekman again, "It is not only adaptive for emotions to be capable of mobilising the organism very quickly (onset), but for the response changes so mobilised not to last very long unless the emotion is evoked again."[26] I shall once again postpone the issue of adaptation. I believe that (as in the case of sudden onset) Ekman has identified a property that is a frequent but not universal property of emotion. It is indeed true, as noted above, that many emotions tend to run their course until they have "spent themselves." Yet it is also true that emotions can last for many years or indeed for a lifetime. Above, I noted the case of vindictiveness. In her story of romantic love (which she denotes by the neologism "limerence"), Dorothy Tennov found that the typical duration of an episode was from eighteen months to three years, with some episodes lasting only a few weeks and others a whole lifetime.[27] The "prejudice emotions," contempt and hatred, can also be very durable. One might ask whether these "standing emotions" are occurrent emotions or simply stable emotional dispositions. In the case of limerence and vindictiveness, at least, I believe they are capable of filling up most of the waking life of the person. In addition to innumerable literary descriptions of love, I can cite Milovan Djilas on revenge:

This land was never one to reward virtue, but it was always strong in taking revenge and punishing evil. Revenge is its greatest delight and glory. Is it possible that the human heart can find peace and pleasure only in returning evil for evil? . . . Revenge is an overpowering and consuming fire. It flares upon and burns away every other thought and emotion. It alone remains, over and above everything else. . . . Vengeance . . . was the glow in our eyes, the flame in our cheeks, the pounding in our temples, the word that had turned to stone in our throats on our hearing that blood had been shed. . . . Vengeance is not hatred, but the wildest and sweetest kind of drunkenness, both for those who must wreak vengeance and for those who wish to be avenged.[28]

Triggered By a Cognitive State

The relation between emotion and cognition is perhaps the central issue in the study of human emotion. As I indicated in section 2.2 above, emotions can be triggered by a large variety of beliefs, relating to others or to oneself and relating to the past, present, or future; they can be held as certain, probable, or merely possible. In addition, emotion can shape cognition, for example, by wishful thinking, and it can itself be the object of cognition, as when we finally notice that we have fallen in love. Because of the intimate relation between cognition and culture, I shall postpone much of what I have to say about these issues to section 4.2 below. Here

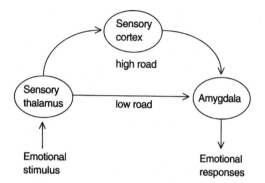

Figure 2.2
Two separate pathways that mediate between sensory signals and
fear reactions (from LeDoux 1996, p. 164).

I shall only discuss some exceptions to the claim that
emotions are invariably triggered by a prior cognitive
assessment or appraisal.

In his work on fear, Joseph LeDoux has shown that
two separate pathways mediate between sensory signals and fear reactions. As indicated in figure 2.2, only
ones of them goes through the part of the brain capable
of making cognitive appraisals.

The other pathway goes directly from the sensory
apparatus to the amygdala, a part of the brain centrally
involved in emotional reactions. The following passage
from LeDoux summarizes some of the differences
between the two pathways:

Although the thalamic system cannot make fine distinctions,
it has an important advantage over the cortical input pathway to the amygdala. That advantage is time. In a rat it takes
about twelve milliseconds for an acoustic stimulus to reach
the amygdala through the thalamic pathway, and almost
twice as long through the cortical pathway. The thalamic
pathway . . . cannot tell the amygdala exactly what is there,

but can provide a fast signal that something dangerous may be there. It is a quick and dirty processing system.

Imagine walking through the woods. A crackling sound occurs. It goes straight to the amygdala through the thalamic pathway. The sound also goes from the thalamus to the cortex, which recognizes the sound to be a dry twig that snapped under the weight of your boot, or that of a rattlesnake shaking its tail. But by the time the cortex has figured this out, the amygdala is already starting to defend against the snake. The information received from the thalamus is unfiltered and biased toward evoking responses. The cortex's job is to prevent the inappropriate response rather than to produce the appropriate one. Alternatively, suppose there is a slender curved shape on the path. The curvature and slenderness reach the amygdala from the thalamus, whereas only the cortex distinguishes a coiled up snake from a curved stick. If it is a snake, the amygdala is ahead of the game. From the point of view of survival, it is better to respond to potentially dangerous events as if they were in fact the real thing than to fail to respond. The cost of treating a stick as a snake is less, in the long run, than the cost of treating a snake as a stick.[29]

In the present state of knowledge, it is hard to assess the importance of these ideas for the study of human emotions. As I noted toward the end of section 2.1 above, in societies that have moved beyond the struggle for survival, major emotional experiences tend to have complex cognitive antecedents. Suppose that I become angry when I hear somebody utter a statement that makes me believe I have been unfairly treated. Barring special cases, it seems implausible that there exists a "low road" by which the auditory input to the thalamus is capable of triggering anger prior to any cognitive processing.[30]

Yet the "low road" may be indirectly important. Suppose that I am standing on the subway platform and another person bumps into me. Before I am able to process the situation cognitively and decide whether the other acted intentionally, recklessly, negligently, or innocently, an angry reaction may be triggered by some "quick-and-dirty" pathway.[31] Supposing that the other was in fact innocent (somebody else bumped into him and made him lose his balance), we may distinguish three cases: First, I recognize that my anger was unwarranted and cease to feel or express anger in any way. I may even apologize for any anger I did express. Second, I recognize that my anger was unwarranted but suppress the awareness and invent another story that justifies my anger. Third, the invention of a story may even preempt the recognition of the other's innocence. Whereas the second scenario is a case of self-deception, the third is one of wishful thinking. In either case, the reluctance to admit (to myself or to others) that I behaved angrily without justification causes me to invent a story that justifies my anger. Hence what I have called "complex cognitive antecedents" of an emotion may themselves be induced by a set of causes that include (1) an emotional reaction without any such antecedents and (2) a self image that would make me uncomfortable thinking that I was capable of reacting angrily without reason. In such cases, the relation between cognition and emotion is both backward and forward—the emotion induces the belief that justifies it—rather than, as in the standard case, merely forward.

LeDoux has shown that the trigger of fear may be sensory or perceptual rather than cognitive. Similarly, the trigger of musical emotion is perceptual rather than cognitive. There are no propositional beliefs that have to be in place before we can experience a given piece of music as sad, joyful, or triumphant. More controversially, *love* may be triggered by perception of a face or a bodily form rather than by any beliefs about the person in question. Stendhal, for instance, is commonly cited as saying that beliefs about the wonderful properties of the other person are the effect of love, through a process he called "crystallization," rather than its cause. Yet although he certainly did make statements to that effect, he also claimed that a necessary condition for love was the belief that the other person might love oneself.[32] This relational belief triggers love, which in turn triggers nonrelational beliefs about the other. The issue is obviously not one that lends itself to easy resolution; I refer the reader to world literature, passim.

Directed Toward an Intentional Object

Emotions, like desires and beliefs, are intentional: they are *about* something. They differ in this respect from other visceral feelings, such as pain, drowsiness, nausea, and vertigo. The analogy with desires and beliefs is often taken very far. Just as we say that a person desires that p be the case or believes that p is the case, where p is some proposition, so it is often asserted that the typical form of statements of emotion is that "X emotes that p."[33] In certain cases, this analysis is accurate enough. I may be ashamed *that* I have done something bad or angry *that* the world is so unfair. Yet I may also be angry *at* or *with* someone—the intentional object being a person rather than a state of affairs. And in the case of hatred or love, the emotion can *only* be stated with a personal object. Envy too is always directed at a person. There are several entries in the *OED* for "I am indignant that . . ." (*and* for "I am indignant with . . .") but none for "I am envious that . . . ."

It is commonly asserted that *moods* such as free-float-
ing anxiety form an exception to the claim that all emotions have intentional objects. Because I do not think we
have a very good understanding of the relation between
occurrent emotions, moods, and emotional dispositions, I prefer to cite the more unambiguous counterexample of musical emotions. As Malcolm Budd writes,

In the case of the musical expression of emotion, the emotion
you are moved by is . . . both abstract and, as it were, disem-
bodied: the emotion is not about any definite state of affairs
and it is not experienced by someone of definite characteristics (age, race, sex, and so on). If the emotion is triumph, it
will be triumph whose object is not specified, and it will be
the triumphant feeling, not of a particular individual, but
only of an indeterminate persona, defined only by the nature
of the emotion. . . . The emotion lacks both a definite object
and a definite subject.[34]

Inducing Physiological Changes ("Arousal")

The subjective intensity of the emotions derives largely
from concomitant physiological arousal. (It also derives
from their valence, further discussed below.) Familiar
symptoms of emotional arousal include pounding of
the heart, loosening of the bowels, lumps in the throat,
nausea, and so on.[35] To some extent, specific emotions
can be linked to specific dimensions of arousal. For the
important special case of autonomic responses, Robert
Levenson reports heart-rate acceleration during anger,
fear, and sadness; heart-rate deceleration during disgust; as well as vascular differences between fear and
anger. He also adds, however, that even with more
research "the final tally of distinctions is likely to be
small."[36]

In some cases we may use the presence of arousal (and valence) to distinguish genuine emotions from superficially similar "quasiemotions." As Robert Gordon observes, the idea of fear lends itself both to a visceral and a nonvisceral interpretation.[37] The former is what I experience when faced with acute danger, the latter what I refer to when I say that I take my umbrella because I fear it might rain. Similarly, attitudes of regret and sympathy may or may not go together with pangs or warm feelings. Yet one should not conclude that arousal is a universal feature of the emotions. Nico Frijda argues that sometimes "there are no signs of autonomic arousal while subjects say they are, or feel, happy or anxious or angry. It is as well to take such subjects at their word, as long as their behavior does not contradict them."[38] Another counterexample is provided by emotions generated by works of art. Although horror movies may generate arousal, the *Goldberg Variations* are less likely to do so.

Having Physiological and Physiognomic Expressions

Emotions have characteristic expressions. They include bodily posture, voice pitch, flushing and blushing, smiling and baring one's teeth, laughing and frowning, weeping and crying. Although, as Frijda says, "A thin line divides expression from true emotional actions,"[39] the distinction can usually be made. Also, although many expressions are very closely related to the physiological responses I have just discussed, some are not. Expressions, by definition, are observable to others, whereas arousal often is not. Some expressions may owe their existence to the fact that they communicate emotion to others, whereas in other cases this effect may be an accidental byproduct that may or may not be adaptive. In a fight, a person might want his adversary to think that he is angry, but not that he is afraid. It is in his interest, therefore, to simulate or suppress the relevant emotional expressions, that is, to fake signs of anger or hide signs of fear. Because these signs are to a considerable extent involuntary, perfect simulation or suppression may be difficult. Yet in social interaction what matters is the ability to fool others, whose capacity to detect imperfect simulation or suppression may itself be far from perfect.[40]

Although fear, anger, joy, and a few other emotions are reliably associated with characteristic facial expressions, this does not seem to be the case for the more complex human emotions. As far as I know, there are no outwardly observable signs that allow us to distinguish guilt from shame, hope from joy, pride from pridefulness, malice from envy, or regret from disappointment. Noel Carroll observes, for instance, that to convey emotion in movies, showing the human face may not be sufficient. "In order to arrive at a more fine-grained and unambiguous characterization of the emotion, we depend on knowing the object or cause of the emotion in question." Hence in editing "that is devoted to conveying the emotional state of a character, we move from the glance to the target, in order to ascertain the particular emotion of the character."[41]

Inducing Specific Action Tendencies

Emotions tend to be associated with specific action tendencies. Guilt induces tendencies to make repairs, to confess, or to punish oneself. The action tendency of shame is to disappear or to hide oneself, and in extreme cases to commit suicide. The action tendency of envy is to destroy the envied object or its possessor. Anger induces a tendency to harm the person who harms one. The action tendency of hatred is to make the object of the emotion disappear from the face of the earth. Although these are all dark or negative emotions, positive emotions also have associated with them typical action tendencies. One action tendency of love, for instance, is to seek out the company of the person who is the object of the emotion. The action tendency of sympathy is to help those who have helped one.

As these examples suggest, action tendencies can have several aims. Given a negative emotion, one often has a tendency to eliminate the conditions that produced it. The person who has cheated on his taxes and sends an anonymous check to the Internal Revenue Service is trying to establish a state of affairs in which he no longer has reason to feel guilty, and the person who destroys the career of a rival is trying to establish a state in which there is nothing to trigger his envy. In other cases, one seeks the restoration of an equilibrium. The angry person who seeks revenge is trying not to undo the harm that was done to him but to create an equilibrium in which harm is matched by harm. The guilty person who reacts by punishing himself is trying not to undo the harm he did but to create an equilibrium in which suffering is matched by suffering.

It is important to emphasize that these are action *tendencies*. Even though we may feel a brief destructive urge at the sight of the greater good of another, most people learn to shrug it off without further action. The urge for revenge too is regularly suppressed in societies that teach the principle of turning the other cheek. The person who is tempted to send a check to the IRS may decide, on reflection, that he would rather keep the money. As these examples suggest, the counterforces that keep action tendencies in check range from self-interest to social norms. I return to this issue in section 4.2.

Not all emotions have action tendencies. Hume asserts, plausibly, that "pride and humility are pure emotions in the soul, unattended with any desire, and not immediately exciting us to action."[42] Also, relief, regret, disappointment, sadness, grief, and most of the aesthetic emotions do not seem to suggest any specific actions. Although small children sometimes want to get on the stage to save the actor from an impending danger, most works of art do not induce any action tendencies in readers, listeners, or viewers. In fact, it has been suggested that the aesthetic emotions have an exceptional purity that is due to their dissociation from action.[43]

Accompanied By Pleasure or Pain ("Valence")

Psychologists use the term "valence" to refer to the fact that emotions are experienced as pleasant or painful, desirable or undesirable, making for happiness or unhappiness. For many twentieth-century city dwellers, this is the most important aspect of the emotions. Although they may have originated as part of the defensive and offensive action systems of the organism and still exhibit that aspect under stressful circumstances, their hedonic aspect is more important in everyday living. The feeling of shame can be unbearably painful, as shown by the suicide of a Navy admiral who was about to be exposed as not entitled to some of the medals he was wearing, or by the suicides in 1997 of six Frenchmen who were caught in a crackdown on pedophilia. Conversely, the radiant love of Anne Elliott at the end of *Persuasion* is unsurpassable happiness. Some emotions are intensely worth striving or wishing for; others intensely worth avoiding.

In the subjective experience of emotion, valence and arousal are usually fused. Analytically, however, they may to some extent be dissociated from each other, as shown by the "mixed emotions," such as nostalgia or the bittersweet emotion we may feel at the sight of a friend's success. If the pleasures from thinking about a good past experience offset the pain from realizing that it is over, or if the pleasures of sympathy offset the pains of envy, the experience may have neutral valence and yet be accompanied by arousal. Thus in an experiment involving interpersonal comparisons, Abraham Tesser was able to induce emotional experiences that were affectively neutral yet had positive arousal, as evidenced by subjects' enhanced ability to perform simple tasks and decreased ability to perform complex tasks.[44] As these findings demonstrate, nonzero (positive or negative) valence is not a universal feature of emotional experiences. Although introspection suggests that pure or elementary experiences are either painful or pleasurable, I do not know about any hard evidence to that effect.

Summary

From this survey I conclude that the features most robustly associated with the emotions are those of unbidden occurrence, cognitive antecedents, intentional objects, arousal, action tendencies, and valence. (I ignore the elusive notion of a unique qualitative feel.) Although the features of sudden onset, brief duration, and characteristic expressions are also frequently observed, they seem to be less central in human emotions than in animal emotions. Yet no single feature is universally observed. The most striking counterexamples are the musical emotions, which do not seem to have any of the putative defining features apart from unbidden occurrence and valence. These two features, however, characterize *all* visceral feelings, and hence cannot capture what is specific to emotion.

2.4   What Emotions Are: Causal Analysis

These conclusions leave us with a confused picture. To make further progress, we could try to go beyond phenomenology and look for the proximate or remote *causes* of emotional reactions. On the one hand, we could search for the neurophysiological pathways by which perception and cognition trigger *occurrent emotions*. On the other hand, we could try to identify the evolutionary mechanisms that produced the various *emotional dispositions*. As far as I can judge, neither approach has yielded anything like a unified understanding of the emotions.

Proximate Causes

Many neurophysiological studies of the emotions fall in the black-box category. There is by now much evidence that many aspects of the emotions that lend themselves to animal experiments—"rage, fear, separation distress, maternal nurturance, anticipatory eagerness, and various facets of sexuality"[45]—are under neurochemical control. To cite an example at random: "Glutamate and its analogues administered directly into the brain can precipitate aggressive rage, as well as fear responses and distress-induced vocalizations. However, it remains to be clearly demonstrated that these behavioral displays are accompanied by internally experienced affect. It remains possible that glutamate-evoked behaviors reflect pseudoaffective motor displays organized at quite a low level of the neuraxis."[46] Yet these studies do not add up to a unified theory. For one thing, they do not address the specifically human emotions. For another, even for the emotions they do address, they do not offer anything like a common mechanism. Rather, they provide the building blocks out of which a mechanism (or mechanisms) may be made.

We know from LeDoux's work on fear what such a mechanism could look like. The basic structure displayed in figure 2.2 can be expanded and refined to include finer differentiations and additional neuronal connections. Although still imperfectly specified, the neural machinery of fear seems to be charted well enough to allow us to assert that we understand the basic mechanisms involved. The amygdala serves as a hub or clearing central that regulates autonomic and behavioral responses, as well as providing feedback to the cortex.[47] In the foreseeable future, the other emotions common to humans and animals—such as rage, distress, maternal feelings, and sexual feelings—will no doubt be charted in a similarly detailed way. We shall then be able to decide whether they rely on the same basic mechanism or whether entirely different systems are involved. LeDoux emphasizes, "There may be many emotions that do not depend upon the amygdala and its connections."[48] More generally, he notes,

To the extent that emotional responses evolved, they evolved for different reasons, and it seems obvious to me that there must be different brain systems to take care of these different kinds of functions. Lumping all of these together under the unitary concept of emotional behavior provides us with a convenient way of organizing things—for distinguishing behaviors that we call emotional (for example, those involved with fighting, feeding, sex, and social bonding) from those that reflect cognitive functions (like reasoning, abstract thinking, problem solving, and concept formation). However, the use of a label, like "emotional behavior," should not necessarily lead us to assume that all of the labeled functions are mediated by one system of the brain. Seeing and hearing are both sensory functions, but each has its own neural machinery.[49]

Even if, however, all the emotions currently studied in laboratory experiments turn out to rely on the same neural machinery, we still would not understand the more complex human emotions. Moreover, I have serious doubts that these are amenable to controlled scientific study, and not simply because of ethical and practical limitations. As I have asserted several times above and will discuss in more detail later, many human emotions depend on complex cognitive antecedents. Moreover, these emotions are also capable of shaping cognition in subtle ways, and thereby altering the emotions themselves. A scientific analysis of these interactions would require the ability to identify the neuronal basis of complex beliefs and the pathways by which they shape and are shaped by emotions. Suppose that I am engaged in a joint venture with another person, who has just pulled off a risky enterprise that benefits us both. Rather than rejoicing in the happy outcome, I react with anger because my envy of his cleverness lends salience to the thought that the outcome *might* have been disastrous. Given the fate of earlier attempts to legislate a priori what science can and cannot explain, it would be foolhardy to assert that a neurochemical analysis of these mental alchemies is impossible *in principle*. Yet success, were it to come, lies so far into the future that the prospect can safely be ignored for now.

It is possible, then, that the category of emotion may turn out to be no more useful for scientific purposes than the categories of animals that live in water or animals that have four legs. As I argued in chapter 1, the latter categories are not entirely useless. Similarly, even if the various emotions are mediated by different neuronal systems, they may have some common phenomenological properties that have convergent causal effects. I return to this question in section 4.2 below. Let me simply mention an example of what I have in mind. In some cultures or subcultures, there is a tendency to condemn "emotional" behaviors that involve losing control and doing what one might regret later. Although these behaviors can be triggered by many different emotions, with entirely different upstream causal histories, they have the common downstream effect of inducing disapproval and shame.

Remote Causes

Even if we do not have a unified theory of *how* emotions
come about, we might have a coherent idea about *why*
they exist. We might, in other words, try to explain emotional dispositions by their biological *functions*. For
some aspects of some emotions, this approach is quite
compelling. The action tendencies of anger and fear
induce states of readiness that enable the organism to
deal with dangers or challenges from the environment.
Emotions of distress in young offspring and the corre-
lated parental emotions are clearly useful from the evolutionary point of view, the former because of their
characteristic expressions and the latter because of the
actions they induce. Yet even in these very basic emotions, it is not clear that all the associated properties
provide an evolutionary benefit. The properties of sudden onset, unbidden occurrence, and brief duration are
obviously useful. The various forms of arousal, by contrast, may actually detract from evolutionary fitness.
Rather than enhancing efficient performance, they may
reduce it. Frijda cites, for instance, "disturbances of
motor co-ordination by trembling and speech difficulties due to a dry mouth."[50] Also, "anecdotes abound
about being unable to move or think when confronted
with danger, or about ineffectual fumbling with oxygen
masks or escape hatches, or about the last match extinguished by the trembling of one's fingers."[51] Similarly,
it is not clear whether the *valence* of these emotions provides an evolutionary benefit.

I need to say a few words about evolutionary explanations more generally. Suppose we find that certain
emotional dispositions are universally observed in

human beings, and perhaps also in specific classes of other animals. It is then tempting to infer that these dispositions exist because they provide reproductive benefits. Before giving in to the temptation, however, it is useful to keep in mind the following provisos.

First, the dispositions may have been useful in the lower species where they first evolved and yet have lost their usefulness in the higher species that evolved subsequently. Thus the alleged ability of the emotions to enhance decision making may to some extent be an artifact of the emotions themselves. The emotions *are* useful, but only because they also undermine other ways of dealing with acute problems.

Second, for a given species, the dispositions may have been useful when they were first established and yet have later lost their usefulness because of changes in the environment. Thus if we find human beings in the grip of emotions that evolved million of years ago, we cannot assume that they remain useful in terms of reproductive fitness. For one thing, in many modern societies the link between ecological fitness (as measured, for instance, by life expectancy) and reproductive fitness has been severed. For another, emotions that did contribute to ecological fitness at earlier stages of humanity need no longer do so. Violent emotional behavior that may have enabled our remote ancestors to assert their dominance may today lead straight to prison. As Frijda notes, "Too much anger in a soccer player earns him a penalty rather than a goal."[52]

Third, even when it first evolved, a given emotional disposition may have arisen as a part or byproduct of a larger complex. The fact of *pleiotropy*—a given genotypical constellation may have many phenotypical expressions—should always be kept in mind. It could well be that a given emotional disposition, taken by itself, detracts from fitness and yet is maintained as part of an evolutionary package solution. As a purely speculative example, *regret* and *disappointment* might fit this category. The proverbial wisdom "Don't cry over spilt milk" reflects the idea that these two emotions are sources of pointless suffering. Yet perhaps—once again, merely as an illustrative conjecture—regret and disappointment are indissociable from *hope*, which does have a useful motivating function.

Fourth, less conjecturally, some of the properties of a given emotional disposition might by themselves detract from fitness and yet be maintained as part of a package solution. Although anger and fear are overall useful dispositions, the arousal they generate may detract from their instrumental efficiency, as we have seen. Some emotional expressions may also have a negative effect, as when visible fear encourages an aggressor. These expressions may, of course, have benefits as well. When an aggressor perceives that I am afraid rather than angry, he may decide to refrain from attack. My claim is not that the negative effects of emotional expression are offset by the positive ones. Rather, it is that even if the negative effects dominate, they may be offset by the positive effects of *other* aspects of the emotion, notably the associated action tendency.

Finally, when assessing the impact of an emotional disposition on reproductive fitness, one has to take account of *all* effects of the disposition, indirect as well as direct. In the case of anger, for instance, it may be true that irascible people often get their way,[53] but that is only part of the story. Others will learn to recognize them as irascible and walk around them rather than have any dealings with them. Sometimes one has no choice, but often one can find alternative and more reasonable partners. Irascible people will find themselves shunned, which detracts from opportunities for mutually favorable interactions with others. They may gain more in each interaction, but they will interact more rarely. They will not, moreover, be able to learn that their emotional disposition works against them, and hence will have no incentive to control themselves. They will get positive reinforcement from their encounters with others—they find that being angry works!—but they cannot get feedback from the encounters they fail to have. I am not saying that the net effect of irascibility is negative, only that one cannot show it to be positive simply by citing a positive impact in isolation from other effects.

I believe that if these caveats were kept more firmly in mind, it would be easier to resist the temptation to seek evolutionary explanations for each and every aspect of each and every emotion. In particular, the more complex human emotions do not seem to lend themselves well to this kind of analysis. I do not doubt that any competent sociobiologist could, on short notice, come up with a "just-so story" about the reproductive benefits of (say) malice, pride, hatred, or "limerence." Yet whether the account relies on the signaling function of the emotions, on their ability to underwrite the credibility of threats and promises, or on their efficacy in sustaining motivation over time, it would just be another story. Modeling always implies simplification. Just-so stories, which often simplify outrageously, can be valuable for the partial insights they provide. Yet when the question is whether a phenomenon exists because of its *net* reproductive benefits or in spite of its *net* reproductive costs, telling a story to demonstrate that it has *some* benefits or costs is not likely to be useful.

Summary

In chapter 1, I argued that emotions stand out among the states capable of affecting human behavior because they are both strongly visceral and strongly cognitive. For the less cognitive states, causal analysis has proved quite successful. As we shall see in the next chapter, we now have something like a unified theory of the proximate causes of addictive cravings. There are also well-developed causal theories of the (almost) entirely visceral states of pain, drowsiness, and the like. In the case of emotions, however, their strong cognitive component is an obstacle to causal analysis. With regard to the search for proximate causes, emotions are prime examples of phenomena in which small changes can have large effects. A person in the grip of "limerence" who learns a minuscule fact about the object of his emotion ("She did not go to the party even though she knew I might be there") may go from ecstasy to misery in a matter of seconds. Such phenomena are notoriously hard to study. With regard to the search for remote causes, the fact that human emotions are embedded in complex networks of social relations makes it very hard to study the net effect of this or that emotional disposition. Overall, causal analysis cannot supplement phenomenology by providing a unified framework for the study of the emotions, at least for the time being.

3   Addiction

3.1   How Do We Know What We Know about Addiction?

As in chapter 2, I begin with introspection. To understand the key addictive phenomena of *craving* and *relapse*, some personal experience is useful. Very many know the temptations of food (on the assumption that compulsive eating counts as an addiction) or the lures of risk taking (if compulsive gambling counts as one). A large fraction of the population in contemporary Western societies have at some time smoked more than they wished they did. The number of individuals who have come close enough to "heavy drinking" or "problem drinking" to understand some of the phenomenology of alcoholism is also substantial. Speaking for myself, I have found that my acquaintance with some of these (putative) addictions helps my thinking about them. The feeling of "letting go" that precedes and facilitates relapse, for instance, is hard to describe to someone who has not experienced it. Conversely, I find it a handicap that because of my risk aversion in financial matters, I cannot get inside the mind of gamblers.

As in the case of emotions, we may supplement intro-spection with fiction and the writings of the moralists. The effects of alcohol and more recently of heroin have been portrayed by many writers, among them William Burroughs. The phenomenology of compulsive gam-bling has been conveyed by Dostoyevsky and Hamsun and, even more strikingly perhaps, by Pascal. In his analysis of *divertissement*, Pascal argues that gambling is one of the activities that people will take up to escape from their existential or metaphysical *ennui*:

This man spends his life without weariness in playing every day for a small stake. Give him each morning the money he can win each day, on condition he does not play; you make him miserable. It will perhaps be said that he seeks the amuse-ment of play and not the winnings. Make him, then, play for nothing; he will not become excited over it and will feel bored. It is, then, not the amusement alone that he seeks, a languid and passionless amusement will weary him. He must get excited over it and deceive himself by the fancy that he will be happy to win what he would not have as a gift on condition of not playing; and he must make himself an object of passion, and excite over it his desire, his anger, his fear, to obtain his imagined end, as children are frightened at the face they have blackened.[1]

Yet these nonscientific sources do not have the same importance as they have for the study of emotion. Addictive phenomena lack the universality of emotion and do not loom large in general treatments of the human condition. Although we find a few remarks in Aristotle to the effect that drink may cause weakness of the will, they do not begin to compare with his very full treatment of emotions. Similarly, the place of addiction in world literature is tiny compared to that of emotion. The main sources of our knowledge about addiction are focused and systematic studies, including animal and human experiments, clinical observations, studies of market behavior, policy analyses, as well as historical and anthropological data.

By and large, animals do not get addicted in the wild, so we cannot draw on field studies. Even in the laboratory, it may take considerable ingenuity to get an animal hooked on an addictive substance. Unlike what is the case for emotions, evolution has not produced specialized circuitry for addictive cravings or addictive behaviors. Instead, addiction results when the reward system of the brain is hijacked by chemical substances that played no role in its evolution. Technically, this statement is not entirely accurate because of the role of endogenous or naturally produced opioids (notably endorphins) in some addictive processes.[2] Yet even though these opioids produce tolerance and dependence when administered in large doses, "this should not be interpreted to mean that we develop tolerance and dependence to our endogenous opioid peptides. They are sequestered and released as needed in very small quantities."[3]

Animal experiments have produced a very fine-grained neurophysiological understanding of the mechanisms involved in chemical addiction. I summarize some of the main results in section 3.4 below. Whenever it has been feasible to carry out similar experiments on human beings, these findings have been confirmed, *without exception*. All the evidence suggests that the basic neurophysiological machinery of chemical addiction is the same in humans and other animals. Yet experiments with humans have also yielded information not available from animals studies. Most obviously, the interaction between addiction and cognition, discussed in section 4.3 below, can only be studied in subjects with the requisite cognitive capacities. More subtly, experiments with humans can produce knowledge that also applies to other animals even if the setup requires the ability to comply with the verbal instructions of the experimenter. For instance, to support their "incentive-sensitization theory of addiction," Terry Robinson and Kent Berridge cite the finding that subjects would self-administer "a low dose of morphine and not the placebo, but reported that neither the drug nor the placebo produced pleasure."[4] Although their theory is intended also to cover animals other than humans, only humans are capable of reporting subjective feelings of pleasure.

Clinical studies too are an important source of information about addiction. By observing which treatments help addicts to quit and which don't, one may also gain insights into the nature of addiction itself. To cite only one example, the relative efficacy of nicotine patches and nicotine gum in smoking cessation can help us identify the relative importance of chemical rewards and psychological rewards from smoking. Gum, like cigarettes, can be taken ad libitum, to alleviate psychological tensions as well as chemical withdrawal symptoms. By contrast, because patches provide a passive and slow system of administration of nicotine to the body, they cannot help the individual to cope with a sudden crisis to which he is used to responding by reaching for a cigarette. Gum is in fact somewhat more effective than patches, which suggests that addiction to cigarettes has psychological as well as a chemical components.[5]

The successes and failures of prevention policies may also illuminate the nature of addiction. An example may be taken from a study that "examined the effects of an experimental Saturday closing of liquor retail stores in Sweden. They found a decline in the number of arrests for drunkenness by about 10% and also a decline in the number of domestic disturbances, as well as in outdoor and indoor assaults. On the other hand, the evaluation did not demonstrate any effect on total consumption of alcohol."[6] These findings are plausibly explained by assuming that a small subgroup of individuals decide on Friday not to drink on Saturday, change their minds on Saturday, but nevertheless abstain if the liquor store is closed on Saturday. To anticipate later discussion, the change of mind might be a preference reversal induced by hyperbolic discounting, a cue-dependence effect induced by the sight of other Saturday drinkers, or disinhibition caused by drinking beer (which was available on Saturdays). Whatever the reason, the theory of "rational addiction" proposed by Gary Becker (see section 5.3 below) does not predict any effect of this kind. If the impact of shorter opening hours on drinking were mediated only by the higher transaction costs of purchasing liquor, as implied by his theory, it would show up in the behavior of *all* consumers, not only in problem drinkers.

Market observations can also provide useful information, notably about legal drugs. According to one view of addiction, the addict's need for a drug is so overpowering that he will do anything to get hold of it. If this idea were correct, the demand for the drug should be very price-inelastic. As a matter of fact, however, consumers are quite sensitive to price changes. I

return to the issue of demand-elasticity or, more generally, reward-sensitivity, in section 5.3 below.

A final source of information is provided by historical
and anthropological studies. These too can provide
counterexamples to theories of addiction that might
seem plausible if attention were restricted to modern
Western societies. Consider, for instance, the idea that
certain genetically vulnerable individuals are very
likely to become alcoholics if they are exposed to alcohol, which implies that any population in which the use
of alcohol is common must contain a subpopulation of
alcoholics. As we shall see in section 4.3 below, these
propositions do not stand up to cross-cultural evidence.
Historical and anthropological studies can also identify
differences between the behavior of (what we would
call) addicts in societies that lack a concept of addiction
and addicts' behavior in societies in which such behavior is conceptualized as addictive.

3.2   What Addictions There Are

If we ask what counts as addiction at the preanalytical
level, we first run into the problem that the English
word "addiction" does not have exact equivalences in
all languages. French or Norwegian, for instance, use
terms such as "dependence," "toxicomania," "intoxicating substances," or even "habit formation." Some
of these terms prejudge theoretical issues that cannot
be decided on the basis of terminology. It should be an
open question, for instance, whether addiction is
always addiction to a *substance* or whether there also
exist addictions to specific *behaviors* (e.g., gambling).
Moreover, within the class of substances it should be

an open question whether addiction can develop only to those that are in some sense toxic or whether there can also be addiction to nontoxic substances (e.g., overeating). Another issue that should not be prejudged on terminological grounds is whether to draw a distinction between an addiction and a bad habit.

We may distinguish between two extreme views regarding the substances or behaviors that have the potential for becoming addictive. At one extreme, in *The Meaning of Addiction* Stanton Peele argues that "addiction may occur with any potent experience."[7] He criticizes, therefore, what he views as "a peculiar anomaly in twentieth-century pharmacology: the search for a nonaddictive analgesic. . . . Having pain, anxiety, or other negative emotional states relieved through a loss of consciousness or a heightened threshold of sensation is a primary component of addictive experiences; for this reason, all effective pain relievers will inevitably be addictive for some people."[8] At another extreme, Avram Goldstein, in his work *Addiction*, limits himself to seven categories of drugs:[9]

• Nicotine
• Alcohol and related drugs (barbiturates and benzodiazepines such as Valium)
• Opiates (opium, morphine, codeine, heroin)
• Psychostimulants (cocaine, amphetamine)
• Cannabis (marijuana, hashish, THC)
• Caffeine
• The hallucinogens (mescalin, LSD, ecstasy, PCP, etc.)

In between these two approaches is Jim Orford's *Excessive Appetites*, which includes not only addiction to these chemical substances but also overeating, compulsive gambling, and extreme sexual behaviors. Various other writers have cited risk taking, work ("workaholics"), TV watching, reading, video games, pyromania, shoplifting, spending money ("credit-card mania"), surfing on the Internet, and emotional experiences as potential objects of addiction or dependence.

These (putative) addictions can be classified in a number of ways. Although the basic distinction between chemical and behavioral addictions is useful,[10] it is neither exclusive nor exhaustive. The nonexclusiveness is shown by the fact that drug users can be addicted to the mere act of consuming and injecting a drug, independently of its pharmacological effects. The nonexhaustiveness is shown by the addictionlike aspects of food consumption[11] and by the possible addictiveness of emotional experiences. We may also distinguish between the potentially addictive consumptions or behaviors that are observed at nonzero levels in all individuals and those that many, perhaps most, members of the population never adopt at all. The former include eating, risk taking, and emotional experiences; the latter all the chemical addictions and many behavioral ones. The distinction is important for relapse-prevention strategies: it is feasible to adopt a policy of zero smoking but not one of zero eating.

3.3 What Addictions Are: Phenomenological Analysis

On the widest definition of addictions, according to which one can become addicted to "any potent experience," they may not have much in common. Suppose, however, that we choose an extensional definition of intermediate inclusiveness, such as the one proposed by Orford. We can then enumerate a number of properties that are common to many addictions:

- Euphoria and pleasure
- Dysphoria and withdrawal
- Craving
- Tolerance
- Cue dependence
- Belief dependence
- Objective harm
- Crowding out
- Mood alterations
- Desire to quit
- Inability to quit
- Denial
- Struggle for self-control
- Relapse

Except for craving and the craving-related phenomena of cue dependence and relapse, none of these features are universal properties of what we pretheoretically identify as addiction. They cannot, therefore, be used to define addiction. Craving, moreover, obtains so widely that any definition that rested on this feature alone would be overinclusive. For purposes of diagnosis and treatment, one could use a pragmatic approach and define something as an addiction if it possesses (say) eight of the thirteen properties.[12] For more theoretical purposes, this procedure is obviously pointless.

Euphoria and Pleasure

Drugs and addictive behaviors have the capacity to induce pleasurable and even euphoric subjective states, which provide a motivation for engaging in the addictive behavior. Some drugs induce pleasurable stimulation, others pleasurable relaxation. Stimulation ranges from the extremes of euphoria produced by crack or intravenous cocaine to the mild elation from coffee. Drinking and smoking allow us to relax, unwind, forget our worries and, in the case of alcohol, see the world in a generally rosy perspective.

Many writers argue that providing pleasure (or "enhancing brain reward") is a universal feature of addictive experiences.[13] Yet if we accept the distinction between "wanting" and "liking" proposed by Terry Robinson and Kent Berridge, organisms sometimes seek out addictive drugs even if they provide no pleasure (or relief from discomfort). There is, they argue, a separate neuronal system that mediates craving for drugs. "Although this neuronal system usually functions in concert with neuronal systems that mediate pleasure ('liking'), in the addict the normal link between these systems is disrupted and pathological levels of 'wanting' become dissociated from 'liking'."[14] I return to the issue in section 3.4 below.

Dysphoria and Withdrawal

Whereas the use of drugs may induce euphoria, abstinence after prolonged use may produce discomfort and dysphoria. In addition to the outwardly visible physiological effects (tremors, sweating, and the like), the psychological anhedonia can be devastating. There is no doubt that symptoms of abstinence are a very common feature in addiction. If they are defined sufficiently broadly, they may even characterize all addictions. Yet on the broader definitions, abstinence symptoms are also observed for many substances or behaviors that one would not normally think of as addictive. For the present purposes, I shall use the terms "preaddictive," "addictive," and "postaddictive" to refer to the states prior to consumption of an addictive drug (or engagement in an addictive behavior), during consumption, and after consumption. If one defines withdrawal symptoms by the property that the postaddictive state is worse than the addictive one, we would have to say that aspirin produces abstinence symptoms. If, however, we define them more narrowly by the property that the postaddictive state is worse than the preaddictive one, this counterintuitive consequence does not follow. But on this narrower definition, some of the chemical drugs usually classified as addictive do not have withdrawal symptoms either. Some of the hallucinogens, in particular, do not induce physiological or psychological withdrawal symptoms.

The last statement must be qualified, however. Looking back at a good LSD experience and knowing that the substance is currently unavailable, one may feel the pain that is often associated with unfulfilled longings. Yet this experience is just a special case of the mechanism cited in chapter 2: "Past happiness augments present misery." Sometimes, it is *worse* to have loved and lost than never to have loved at all, in the sense that the state succeeding love may be worse than the one that preceded it, yet we do not think of the aftermath of love as inducing abstinence symptoms. If we use a narrow definition of withdrawal that excludes both the reduction of well-being below the addictive state and the memory-induced reduction of well-being below the preaddictive state, there are prima facie addictive phenomena that do not produce withdrawal symptoms. And if we do not want—and I don't think we should want—to say that the cessation of aspirin intake and of love induces withdrawal, we should in fact use the narrow definition.

Craving

All addictive behaviors seem to go together with some form of craving. The idea of craving—the most important explanatory concept in the study of addiction—is complex. If viewed hedonically, it includes the "pull" of euphoria as well as the "push" from dysphoria. Robinson and Berridge argue, however, that craving may be dissociated from hedonic experiences. In their view, craving is based on the *incentive salience* of stimuli rather than on their actual or anticipated hedonic properties. "Stimuli that are attributed with incentive salience become attractive and demand attention. Like the sight of food to a starving person, they cannot be ignored. This does not necessarily make them 'liked'; the sight of food may be irresistibly attractive to the starving person, but if out of reach may torment rather than please. But the food is still very much 'wanted'."[15]

Robinson and Berridge's view is intended to supplement rather than to replace the traditional view, according to which craving is due to hedonic pull or push. Although they define craving in nonhedonic terms, they do not dispute that positive and negative hedonic factors play a role in drug-seeking behavior.[16] The relative importance of these factors varies. For a given drug there may be "considerable variation both among patients and within the same patient over time."[17] There is also variation across different drugs: "The meaning attributed to the word *craving* differs between cocaine abusers and opiate and alcohol abusers. O'Brien, Childress and McLellan surveyed cocaine-dependent individuals and found that they tended to label as craving the positive (high-like) qualities of the cocaine intoxication experience. In contrast, opiate-and-alcohol dependent subjects were more likely to refer to the negative, withdrawal-associated features of these respective substances."[18] The horribly anhedonic state of cocaine withdrawal does not induce any desire for the drug at all. The craving for cocaine, in fact, is often highest immediately after drug administration, when the drug is producing euphoria rather than dysphoria.

Independently of whether craving is an urge to achieve euphoria or to avoid dysphoria, the experience of craving itself—before the urge is satisfied—can be either pleasant or unpleasant.[19] When you come home after a long day at work, the desire for a cigarette or a drink is pleasurable because you know it is about to be fulfilled. Even if the reason I crave a cigarette is that I am at edge because I have been prevented from smoking all day, merely knowing that a cigarette is about to be made available will reduce the dysphoria. If for some reason the craving is not satisfied, it becomes dysphoric.[20] If I believe that the craving is and will remain unsatisfied, it may then subside.

Cravings can also be induced by what we may call the *secondary rewards from addiction*. To explain this idea, let me recall my own experience as a former heavy smoker who quit almost 30 years ago when my consumption reached 40 cigarettes a day. Even today I vividly remember what it was like to organize my whole life around smoking. When things went well, I reached for a cigarette. When things went badly, I did the same. I smoked before breakfast, after a meal, when I had a drink, before doing something difficult, and after doing something difficult. I always had an excuse for smoking. Smoking became a ritual that served to highlight salient aspects of experience and to impose structure on what would otherwise have been a confusing morass of events. Smoking provided the commas, semicolons, question marks, exclamation marks, and full stops of experience. It helped me to achieve a feeling of mastery, a feeling that I was in charge of events rather than submitting to them.[21] This craving for cigarettes amounts to a desire for order and control, not for nicotine.

Drinking too is sustained in part by the secondary rewards it offers. Having a drink can serve the same organizing functions as taking a cigarette. Also, through what Claude Steele and Robert Josephs call "alcohol myopia"—the tendency of alcohol to induce a focus on more salient cues at the expense of cues that are more difficult to retrieve—drinking may provide *the secondary reward of higher self-esteem*. When we drink, we may temporarily lose access to the background knowledge that normally inhibits overvaluation of the self. They cite a study in which the experimenters

had subjects rate the personal importance of 35 trait dimensions and their "real" and "ideal" standing on each dimension both before and after they were made intoxicated or had consumed a placebo drink. . . . They found that getting drunk significantly inflated the self, *but only on traits that were both important to subjects and for which, before drinking, they had acknowledged that their "real" self was considerable worse than their "ideal" self.* . . . Placebo drinks caused no change on any traits. . . . Alcohol may bring [an aspiring person] so close to his ideal state . . . as to make the drug powerfully reinforcing psychologically, and if he continues to seek this reinforcement, even physiologically addictive.[22]

As the last remarks indicate, what I call secondary rewards need not be secondary in a chronological or causal sense. They are secondary only in that they involve cognitive components that we would not observe in animal addiction.

Tolerance

Tolerance is the phenomenon that, as time passes, the agent needs more of a given substance (or activity) to obtain the same subjective experience or, equivalently, that a given dose has a reduced effect. Tolerance can also obtain for nonhedonic effects of drugs, notably for their lethality. The regular heroin dose of a heavy user would be lethal to the novice or to the previously heavy user who has abstained for some time. Acute tolerance may develop within a given episode of consumption, whereas chronic tolerance is a result of prolonged use. Whereas acute hedonic tolerance is well documented, the existence and magnitude of long-term hedonic tolerance is more controversial.[23]

With regard to the behavioral addictions, the question of tolerance is not well understood. Although there is an observed tendency for heavy gamblers to raise the stakes, the odds, or both, it is not clear that this tendency reflects tolerance with regard to the thrills of gambling. The escalation might also be due to the need to make larger and riskier gambles in order to repay old debts. But suppose that it is true that the nature of the "action" in gambling has "an uncanny similarity to 'tolerance' among alcohol, barbiturate, and narcotics addicts. Once the 'high' of a five-hundred-dollar event has been reached, the two-dollar bet no longer achieves the desired effect."[24] We still cannot conclude that there is tolerance. The escalation might originally be caused by the need to repay debts and then sustained by a contrast effect. Before you've experienced the best, you're happy with the second best, but once you've been exposed to the best, perhaps by accident, there is little thrill to be got from the second best. Although the contrast effect and the phenomenon of tolerance are superficially similar, the underlying causal mechanisms are quite different.

Cue Dependence

Craving, withdrawal, and tolerance are produced not only by consumption of drugs. They may also be produced by exposure to a setting in which drugs have been consumed.[25] Even after years of abstinence, an environmental cue traditionally associated with consumption may trigger a number of drug-related responses.[26] Some cue-dependent effects mimic the effects produced by the drug, notably by inducing euphoria. Other cue-dependent effects work in the opposite direction of the normal drug effect.[27] Addicts can develop instant withdrawal symptoms upon re-

turning to a setting in which they have used drugs in
the past. Tolerance too may be cue-dependent. Thus
"an organism is at risk for overdose when the drug is
administered in an environment that, for that organism,
has not previously been extensively paired with the
drug."[28]

Relapse is frequently due to cue conditioning,
whether it takes the form of a conditioned craving for
the drug or of a need to be relieved of conditioned withdrawal symptoms. Thus Avram Goldstein cites

a convincing story from a colleague who had been a nicotine
addict but hadn't smoked for years. He had abstained from
cigarettes in a variety of situations where he had smoked in
the past, and thus he had desensitized himself to a variety of
conditioned associations—cigarettes at parties, cigarettes at
morning coffee, cigarettes at the desk, and so on. One day he
went to the beach and was suddenly overwhelmed by an
intense craving to smoke. He found this beyond understanding until he realized that smoking on the beach had been an
important pattern at one time in his life, and that he had not
had the opportunity to eliminate that particular conditioned
association.[29]

Belief Dependence

Whereas cue-dependent craving is triggered by a sensory signal, craving may also be triggered by the *belief*
that a drug is available, even if neither the drug itself
nor cues signaling its presence are actually given to the
senses. In the same place Goldstein remarks, "Contrary
to what most people might think, craving is not pro-
voked by the absence of the drug to which a person was
addicted, but by its presence—that is, by its availability.
This is illustrated by the nicotine addict who goes skiing

for a whole day, leaving cigarettes behind. No thought is given to cigarettes—they are simply unavailable. Then back at the lodge, where nicotine is available again, intense craving strikes, and the addict lights up." Whereas the beachgoer's craving was triggered by (visual, auditory, or olfactory) *perceptions*, that of the skier was triggered by a *belief* that nicotine was available. Conversely, as noted above, his belief that cigarettes were unavailable while he was out skiing was sufficient to reduce his craving—a phenomenon that has a general similarity to the "sour grapes" mechanism.[30] Note that belief dependence cannot arise in animals incapable of forming beliefs of the requisite complexity.

Objective Harm

Addiction can ravage lives and communities. This is perhaps the most striking aspect of the phenomenon and is the main reason why it has become such an important policy issue. In the United States between three and four hundred thousand people die prematurely from smoking-related diseases each year. As for alcohol, it "has become the nation's most costly health problem. . . . When the cost of lost production, crime and accidents due to alcohol are totaled and added to the cost of treating alcohol addiction . . . , the bill comes to over $117 billion a year."[31] There may be between 1 and 4 million compulsive gamblers in the United States, with the total sums involved ranging up to $90 billion a year.[32] In contemporary Western societies, the need for money to feed a heroin or cocaine habit is responsible for numerous crimes. The enormous profits to be made by selling these drugs, combined with the legal prohibition of the most profitable ones, trigger large amounts of violence, which in turn cause political pressures for severe sentencing of drug crimes. Drugs contribute powerfully to innercity subcultures of poverty.[33] Yet objective harm cannot serve as a defining characteristic of addiction. Coffee addiction, for instance, is essentially harmless.[34]

Crowding Out

Many drugs have a tendency to crowd out all other activities. This may be a constant feature of the addict's life, or occur mainly within individual episodes or binges. The life of the alcoholic or heroin addict revolves around getting the next drink or the next fix: little else matters. Similarly, for the compulsive gambler, all social and professional activities are subordinated to gambling and raising money for gambling. As noted, the urgency in the gambler's case may be due to the need for large winnings to pay back his debts, as well as to a need for the thrill of gambling itself. Bingeing occurs mainly with crack addiction, food disorders, and gambling. Although crowding out is sometimes used to define addiction,[35] smoking and caffeine addiction are compelling counterexamples. When crowding out does occur, the neglect of other considerations is still a matter of degree. In section 5.3 below I discuss whether the craving for drugs can become so dominant that all other concerns are completely bracketed.

Mood Alteration

Apart from the euphoric psychological effects that constitute one main reason for craving them, drugs have other mood effects that can affect the behavior of the addict. The phenomenon may be a short-term (within-episode) effect or a long-term effect. Nicotine and caffeine may enhance short-term mental alertness. Alcohol has clear short-term disinhibitory effects, making people do things they would not do when sober. Among the findings that Steele and Josephs use to support their theory of alcohol myopia is a striking laboratory example in which the researchers

recruited male subjects for a pain-perception/reaction-time experiment and after allowing them to ingest either alcohol or placebo drinks, they gave each subject a noxious tone (through earphones) that subjects believed was delivered by another "partner" subject. The actual subject was to stop the tone by giving the partner an electrical shock as fast as possible. The intensity and duration of this retaliation measured subjects' aggression. The partner, of course, was not a real person but a computer that in the critical condition, matched the subjects's shock with a second noxious tone of equal intensity and duration—an "eye for an eye." Clearly, the smart thing to do in this condition was to give one's partner only a mild shock, and then one would get only a mild one in return. But to be smart, one has to be mindful of the tone contingency. In a nutshell, the sober subjects played it smart, giving very little shock in this eye-for-an-eye condition, whereas the intoxicated subjects plunged ahead, giving nearly three times as much shock. Presumably, the myopia experiences by the intoxicated subjects allowed them access to the provoking stimuli, because of their immediacy and salience, but blurred their appreciation of the delayed inhibiting contingencies, allowing them to be more aggressive than their sober cohorts by a factor of 7 standard deviations.[36]

Another effect of alcohol myopia is that resolutions to stop drinking after a few drinks may dissolve in alcohol. Through the same mechanism, alcohol may trigger relapse in smokers who are trying to quit.[37] Some hallucinogens induce near-psychotic states ("bad trips"). It has been argued that "cocaine may be more of a mood enhancer than a mood elevator," making an initially bad mood worse and a good one better.[38] Long-term effects of cocaine use include personality changes, irritability, anxiety, and paranoia.[39] Gamblers in the final stage of desperation "are never relaxed, but [show] restlessness, irritability, paranoia, hypersensitivity."[40] Claims that chronic marijuana use induces durable personality changes, notably by undermining general motivation, seem unsupported.[41]

Desire to Quit

When addicts come to believe that they are harming themselves by the addictive behavior, they may decide that, all things considered, they would be better off were they not addicted. The desire may take a strong or weak form. In the weak form, the addict wishes he had never started. In the strong form, he wishes to stop. The weak desire does not imply the strong one, for two reasons. First, because of withdrawal effects there are usually high transition costs of going from the addicted state to the nonaddicted state. Second, by the time the addict comes to wish he had never started on the addictive path, his life may be so destroyed that it can never become as good as it was before he got hooked. At this stage, his best option may be to remain addicted. The addict may not even form a weak desire to quit if he fails to recognize that he is harming himself, or recognizes the harm but believes it is justified by the benefits.

Inability to Quit

As a feature characterizing addiction, the desire to quit is important only in conjunction with the inability to quit. The inability has an important time dimension in that it may be either a "within episode" phenomenon or a "between episode" phenomenon. Jellinek draws a distinction between "gamma alcoholism," characterized by "loss of control," and "delta alcoholism," characterized by "inability to abstain." With the latter, "There is no ability to 'go on the water wagon' for even a day without the manifestation of withdrawal symptoms; the ability to control the amount of intake on any given occasion, however, remains intact."[42] Similar distinctions apply to overeating, cocaine addiction, and gambling, but not to smoking or opiates. There are few out-of-control "binge smokers."

The phrase "inability to quit" is deceptively simple.[43] Orthodox Jews regularly resist withdrawal in order to give up smoking during the Sabbath.[44] Alcoholics "can" stop drinking when they are on disulfiram, which makes them ill if they take a drink. It is not clear, however, that this effect is a matter of being sensitive to incentives, so that a strong craving is offset by strong penalties. Rather, *the craving itself seems to subside* when satisfying it would incur sanctions. Many heavy smokers do not find it particularly difficult to abide by airline regulations against smoking yet avidly reach for a cigarette once they are out of the plane. As we saw, cravings may also subside when the drug is thought to be unavailable. Cravings are not only cue-dependent and belief-dependent, but also "cost-dependent."

Denial

Many addicts deny that they have a problem or, if they admit it, deny that they can do anything about it. Here are some of the stock phrases of addictive thinking:[45]

- I am only a social drinker.
- I can quit any time I want to.
- I don't seem to have gained that much weight.
- Just one cigarette can't make a difference.
- I'll make up my losses in the next race.
- I'll quit tomorrow.
- It wouldn't be polite to my hosts if I refused to have dessert.
- Air pollution is more dangerous than smoking.

Addicts often confuse cause and effect, saying, for instance, that they drink because of a marital problem when it is actually the other way around.[46] Although alcoholics and gamblers may be especially prone to deceive others in order to get to the next drink or the next gamble or to explain away what they have done, they also tend to deceive themselves. More generally, the addict can respond to his predicament in one of three ways: by escaping from his awareness of it, by denying it, and by trying to quit. The alcoholic, for instance, may drown his guilt in alcohol, affirm that he is only a social drinker, or join the Alcoholics Anony-

mous. The first two responses obey the pleasure principle, the last the reality principle.

Struggle for Self-control

Many addicts have two strong desires: the desire to consume and the desire to stop consuming. In the struggle
for self-control, now the one, now the other desire
seems to be gaining the upper hand. The most effective
strategies for self-control seem to be private rules[47] and
strategies of precommitment.[48] Whichever technique is
used, we observe a qualitative change in addictive
behavior from the moment when self-control becomes
important. A person who eats too much may be overweight and not too worried about it. From the moment
he forms the desire to be slim and goes on a diet, his
temporal weight profile changes from a steady if slow
upward trend to one that has a steady downward trend
(anorexia), exhibits short-term fluctuations (binge
eating), or shows long-term fluctuations (weight lost
through dieting that is then regained). The transition
from being a heavy drinker to a self-acknowledged
problem drinker triggers similar changes. At the same
time, a number of deceptive and self-deceptive mechanisms come into play. *Ambivalence* is a hallmark of serious addiction in humans.

Relapse

Even when the battle for self-control seems to be won,
there may be a reversal of fortune. Relapse rates are
high for all the major addictions. Typically, relapse follows weeks or months after the beginning of abstinence,

but much longer periods are also observed. A person may succeed in giving up cigarettes and stay away from them for twenty years, only to relapse in a crisis. Typically, consumption in these cases escalates much more rapidly than when the person began to consume in the first place; hence *relapse should not be characterized as readdiction.* As mentioned earlier, cue dependence has a major role in relapse, but it is not the only factor. Stress is also known to trigger relapse, in animals as well as in humans.

Summary

As mentioned earlier, *craving* and craving-related phenomena constitute the common phenomenological core of the addictions. Yet a definition of addiction solely in terms of craving would be too wide to be useful. I might have a craving for butter, for instance, give it up because of the associated risk of heart disease, and relapse when a waiter places a jar of butter and a loaf of bread before me. Yet this syndrome does not warrant a claim that I am addicted to butter. By adding *withdrawal* symptoms to the common core of the addictions, the counterintuitive implication that butter is addictive would be avoided. Yet since (1) some of the putative addictive drugs do not produce withdrawal symptoms, (2) "animals will avidly self-administer a variety of drugs into brain regions that do not produce withdrawal symptoms,"[49] and (3) withdrawal is poorly documented for behavioral addictions such as compulsive gambling,[50] this improved definition will not do either. And although *ambivalence* may be a core feature of serious addiction in humans, it is not present in all human

addictions (very few coffee drinkers show ambivalence) and is largely absent from animal addiction.

3.4 What Addictions Are: Causal Analysis

Although there is still much that is unknown about the
chemical addictions at the physiological level, they do
seem to form a reasonably homogeneous category.
Unlike the emotions, the chemical addictions are a natural kind. As little is known about the physiology of the
behavioral addictions, they will be ignored in the following.

Hedonic effects and other effects of drugs of abuse on
the body arise in four ways. First, there are the *primary
effects*, which arise prior to any learning or habituation.
Second, there are the *feedback effects*, which arise to com-
pensate for the primary effects. Third, there are the *feedforward effects*, which arise to preempt the primary
effects or the feedback effects. Fourth, there are long-
term habituation or *sensitization effects.* Many phenomenological aspects of addiction arise through a combina-
tion of these physiological mechanisms. Others are due
to psychological mechanisms that are common to
chemical and behavioral addictions, and are further
discussed in section 4.3 below.

Primary Effects

It is useful to distinguish between the hedonic effects of
drugs and "nonhedonic" effects. (The term *nonhedonic*
implies not that these effects have no hedonic aspect
but only that they do not arise through the brain-reward
system that generates the hedonic effects.) Whereas the

hedonic effects of the different addictive drugs all seem to arise in pretty much the same fashion, the nonhedonic effects of different drugs emerge through mechanisms that often have little in common with each other.

The primary hedonic effect of a drug is pleasure or euphoria. Until recently, it has been widely accepted that all the major chemical drugs produce euphoria in the same way, by increasing the amount of the neurotransmitter dopamine in the synaptic clefts in a specialized part of the brain. With some drugs, the increase occurs because the drug causes more dopamine to be released, with others because it prevents it from being reabsorbed. Recently some scholars have argued that dopamine mainly serves to focus the attention of the organism to impending reward rather than to produce the experience of the reward itself.[51] According to Robinson and Berridge, for instance, dopamine is involved in "wanting" rather than in "liking." As this view seems not to have replaced the conventional wisdom, I have found it more prudent, as a nonspecialist, to go with the traditional view.

Primary nonhedonic effects vary widely across drugs. With heroin, there is an analgesic (pain-reducing) effect, an effect on the digestive system inducing constipation, and an effect on the respiratory system that can lead to death from overdose. With alcohol, there is a sedative effect on the central nervous system, a disinhibitory effect, an effect on the gastrointestinal tract that may lead to cirrhosis of the liver, and an effect on motor performance. With nicotine, there is an alertness effect and an effect on the vomiting center. With cocaine, there is a stimulant effect on the central nervous system, an anesthetic effect on the mucous membranes of eyes, nose, and throat, and a negative effect on concentration and judgment. Many of the nonhedonic effects may be regarded as costs that addicts are willing to pay to get the hedonic benefit. In some cases, they are not aware of these effects, or only become aware of them when it is too late. Some of them, like the alertness effect of nicotine, can be seen as a side bonus that may (or may not) contribute to the reinforcing effect of the drug.[52]

Feedback Effects

Many drug effects are subject to homeostatic mechanisms by which the body adjusts its functions to reduce or eliminate the deviation from equilibrium. The constipating and analgesic effects of heroine, for instance, are attenuated over time, as is the sleep-inducing effect of barbiturates. Initial hedonic effects also tend to become weaker after repeated use. Robinson and Berridge suggest, however, that apparent hedonic tolerance may to some extent be an artifact of tolerance to nonhedonic effects: "Why then do addicts typically escalate their dose? A possible alternative explanation to tolerance of euphoria is that addicts increase dose to achieve the more intense (and more desirable) subjective effects produced by larger doses. They are able to do his only because tolerance develops to the aversive 'side effects' of drugs."[53] Yet they also assert that there is probably some nonspurious tolerance to the hedonic effects.

It is misleading to think of the feedback as a simple attenuation of the original effect, on the model of habituation to loud noise. Rather, feedback occurs by establishing a new and oppositely directed process that

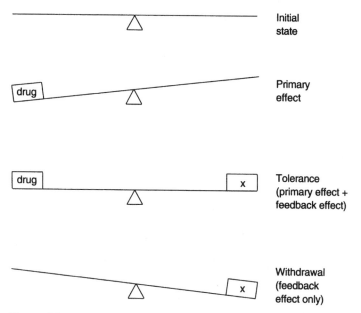

Figure 3.1
Seesaw model of dependence (from Goldstein 1994, p. 82).

partly or wholly eliminates the effect of the original drug action. Although the secondary process cannot be observed directly as long the drug is consumed, it is unmasked and directly observable upon cessation. Once the addict stops consuming the drug, the primary effect will disappear, but the opposing effect may continue for a while. A heroin user, for instance, will suffer diarrhea and hyperalgesia (extreme sensitivity to pain) during withdrawal. A barbiturate user who began using barbiturates to sleep and is now in withdrawal will experience more severe sleep problems than those for which the drug was originally taken. Similarly, hedonic drug effects are weakened by homeostatic mechanisms that reduce the amount of dopamine in the synaptic cleft. When the drug is taken away and these mechanisms remain in place, severe dysphoria can follow. Following Avram Goldstein,[54] we may think of this as the *seesaw model of dependence* (see figure 3.1).

Feedforward Effects

By mechanisms of classical conditioning, the organism can learn to anticipate the effects of drug consumption and in fact produce the effects before consumption takes place. Through such "feedforward effects," the organism responds "not to disturbances, but to stimuli that have been associated with disturbances in the past."[55] Cue dependence, for instance, is a form of feedforward effect. Yet if we ask exactly how the cue dependence triggers craving and in many cases relapse, a puzzling ambiguity emerges. There are, in fact, two kinds of feedforward effects.[56] On the one hand, there are *drug-opposite* conditioned responses, such as conditioned withdrawal and conditioned tolerance. For instance, "when [an] opioid was given without warning by an infusion (unsignaled), the subjects showed a significantly greater physiological response to the drug than when the same dose was 'expected' (self-injected)."[57] When the drug is self-injected, the drug-opposite effect is *subtracted* from the primary effect to produce tolerance. On the other hand, there are *druglike* conditioned responses, such as conditioned euphoria (the "needle freak" phenomenon) and drug placebo effects. When this mechanism operates, the druglike effect is *added* to the primary effect to produce (one form of) sensitization.

Although the existence of oppositely directed cue reactions is not in doubt, there is no full consensus about the conditions under which the one or the other occurs.[58] Yet for the purpose of explaining behavior, the question is not necessarily a crucial one. Exposure to the usual circumstances and paraphernalia of drug taking can trigger craving and relapse *either* through conditioned withdrawal or through conditioned euphoria. On the one hand, "animal and human data suggest that stimulants such as amphetamine and cocaine are more likely to produce drug-like conditioned responses while opioids in human subjects produce more prominent drug-opposite responses."[59] On the other hand, there is the finding (mentioned earlier) that cocaine-dependent individuals tend to label as craving the positive qualities of the cocaine intoxication, whereas opiate-and-alcohol dependent subjects were more likely to refer to the negative features of these respective substances. These two findings together suggest that exposure to drug-related cues may trigger cravings regardless of the precise mediating mechanism. In cocaine addicts, cues trigger euphoria and hence craving. In heroin addicts, cues trigger dysphoria and hence craving.

Sensitization

There is increasing evidence that prolonged drug use has irreversible effects on the brain that leave ex-addicts highly vulnerable to relapse. Although within-episode consumption usually shows tolerance to drugs, across-episode consumption may display sensitization, so that smaller doses are needed to produce a given effect. This mechanism is well documented with respect to behavioral effects of various drugs, for example, the ability of amphetamine or morphine to induce locomotor hyperactivity or stereotyped behavior.[60] Moreover, there is evidence of sensitization to the reinforcing effects of drugs.[61] According to one line of argument, repeated exposure to drugs has two separate effects on the dopamine system in the brain.[62] On the one hand, it induces a durable reduction of the level of dopamine production during drug-free states. Former addicts may be subject to a permanent state of low-level dysphoria, being in that respect similar to individuals who are born with a "reward-deficiency syndrome."[63] On the other hand, chronic drug administration increases the amount of dopamine that a given dose of the drug will release into the synaptic cleft.

Summary

It would be inaccurate to say that all chemical addictions are generated and maintained by identical causal mechanisms. The nonhedonic effects that play an important role for many aspects of addiction involve very different brain processes. The hedonic effects, although more homogeneous in their origin, arise in different parts of the brain reward system. Yet these observations should not be allowed to overshadow the essentially uniform nature of the chemical addictions. They arise because of the ability of drugs to affect the operation of neurotransmitters in the dopaminergic system, increasing the amount of dopamine in the synaptic cleft. By mechanisms that remain controversial, dopamine induces the craving that is the central feature of drug-taking behavior. If sustained over time, the same behavior induces neuroadaptation, notably withdrawal symptoms (anhedonia). These effects may also be produced prior to actual drug consumption, as a result of conditioned learning. Once we step back from the myriad of differences in detail, there is an impressive similarity across the handful of addictive drugs. The most compelling proof of basic uniformity of drug action is perhaps *cross-priming*:

Thus, priming doses of morphine reinstate cocaine self-administration and priming doses of amphetamine or the dopamine antagonist bromocriptine reinstate heroin-trained responding. In this reviewer's opinion, such cross-priming of drugs between drugs of different classes speaks powerfully to the existence of *common* neurobiological and *common* neuropharmacological substrates for the actions of abusable substances with the dopamine reward circuitry of the brain.[64]

4

Culture, Emotion, and Addiction

4.1 The Concept of Culture

With an important qualification to be stated below, I shall understand culture as any pattern of behavior, norms, values, beliefs, and concepts that is more than individual but less than universal. Culture is the realm of the particular. Although anthropologists often use the term in a more restrictive sense, to denote specific practices (e.g., rituals), beliefs systems (e.g., myths), or values (e.g., taboos), this is not the only way in which it is used. The frequent references to "business culture," "youth culture," "political culture," and so on, suggest that culture can be seen as a characteristic pattern of any group whatsoever. This, at any rate, is how I shall use the term here.

Coordination Equilibria

As a first approximation, culture includes all patterns of human *behavior* that are constant (or frequent) within a certain human group but are not found (or are found less frequently) in other groups. In the context of the present work, for instance, we may talk about "cultures of envy" or "cultures of drinking." In some groups, destructive behavior induced by envy is common. As a corollary, behavior motivated by the desire to avoid triggering the envy of others also becomes frequent. In other groups these behaviors occur less frequently. In Nordic countries, a main pattern of drinking behavior is heavy consumption of hard liquor on weekends. In Latin countries, this pattern is much less frequent. Instead, we often find a pattern of daily consumption of wine that is rarely observed in Nordic countries. Although the incidence of cirrhosis of the liver might be the same in both patterns, the former typically generates more violence.

This characterization of culture is obviously incomplete. It contains no reference to the norms, values, and beliefs that are usually thought of as an integral part of culture and that can play an essential role in sustaining the behaviors that differentiate one human group from another. Before I proceed to discuss these aspects of culture, let me note that differences in norms, values, and beliefs are not a necessary concomitant of behavioral differences. *Language* provides a striking example. If two groups exhibit different linguistic behaviors (i.e., speak different languages), there is no reason why their practice should be sustained by beliefs about the superiority of their own language and the inferiority of the other. Although some group members may indeed entertain beliefs of this kind, this is not in general what makes them stick to their own language. Rather, they do so because a language is a *coordination equilibrium*. If I want to be understood by other members of my group, I'd better speak the language we all use rather than a foreign one. A useful contrast is provided by linguistic differences within the larger group. If speakers of English differ in their syntax and pronunciation, it is not only because of a need to make themselves understood. In some cases and to some extent, the differences are due to social norms that stigmatize other variants of the language as inferior.

This distinction between social norms and coordination equilibria goes back at least to Max Weber.[1] In theory, it is clear enough. Behavior guided by social norms is sustained by the desire to avoid the disapproval of others. Behavior that conforms to a coordination equilibrium is sustained by self-interest, since "the person who does not adapt himself to it is subjected to both petty and major inconveniences and annoyances as long as the majority of the people he comes in contact with continue to uphold the custom and conform to it."[2] A pure example of the latter case is not easy to find, however. The standard example of driving on the right side of the road is somewhat imperfect, since those who unilaterally drive on the left not only run the risk of an accident, but also expose themselves to the disapproval of other drivers. The reason—which holds quite generally for coordination equilibria—is that each actor not only wants to drive on the right as long as others do, but also wants others to drive on the right as long as he does. If one actor deviates, he may not only risk harm to himself but also risk harming others, who will react with disapproval. In some cases, though, the harm that the deviation imposes on others may be so small or hard to notice that the actor only incurs practical inconvenience to himself without any disapproval.

Social Norms

In some cases, then, social norms are backup systems for coordination equilibria. They add fear of disapproval to self-interest as a motivation for choosing the equilibrium behavior. In other cases, social norms stand by themselves as the only motivation for behavior. It has been widely argued that they can help group members overcome problems of collective action and, moreover, that their presence can be explained by this effect.[3] Rather than reinforcing self-interest, these norms are said to counteract self-interest and to induce behavior that is desirable for the group as a whole. Alleged examples include norms of vengeance as a means of population control, norms against rate busting among workers as a means of preventing the firm from exploiting them, norms against spitting in the streets as a means of containing contagious diseases, and norms against displaying one's wealth as a means of ensuring social cohesion. As I have argued elsewhere,[4] these functionalist arguments are often dubious. The beneficial consequences of the norms are not always convincingly demonstrated, and the feedback mechanism by which the consequences sustain the norms is rarely specified. I do not want to say that there are no such norms, only that there is little hard evidence to support the functionalist claims.

In addition to norms that reinforce self-interest and those that promote group interest at the expense of self-interest, there are norms that serve the interest of one subgroup at the expense of another. Norms of equality, for instance, serve the interest of those who are badly off at the expense of those who are well off. In hierarchical societies, norms of deference serve the upper tiers of the social system at the expense of the lower ones. I assume that norms are held by those whom they harm as well as by those whom they benefit. Hence, in my terminology, the statement "Children should be seen and not heard" does not express a social norm unless it is one to which children also subscribe.[5] When adults enforce this principle merely through their power to punish children, we are dealing with a very different phenomenon from what we observe when members of a subordinate class police each other to ensure the proper deference to their superiors. In the latter case, but not in the former, emotions also come into play (see section 4.2).

Finally, there are many norms that make little utilitarian sense from an individual, group, or subgroup perspective. Norms of language, dress, etiquette, and the like, fall in this category. Norms against sticking one's neck out do not benefit anyone in any material sense, nor do various norms limiting the use of money (e.g., the norm against paying a person to get his place in a bus queue). Codes of honor, norms of vengeance, and similar phenomena also fail to bring about any benefits to those who subscribe to them. An obvious objection to these claims is that since those who deviate from the norm risk being punished or ostracized by other members of the group, abiding by it provides the straightforward benefit of not being penalized. Yet because this benefit is conceptually tied to the existence of the norms, the objection does not allow us to assimilate this set of norms to cases in which the benefits are independently valuable.

Values

A culture is also characterized by a specific set of values. Although norms and values are normative concepts and are often closely linked to each other, they also differ in important ways. Values, as I understand them here, are matters of individual preference and commitments.[6] To the extent that they are part of a culture, they are shared with others rather than being idiosyncratic. This does not imply, however, that their observance is regulated by the disapproval of others. Many people abide by moral and religious values because of a personal commitment, not because they are afraid of what others would say if they didn't. Although they may have learned these values from their parents and may well stick to them partly because they ask themselves "What would my parents have thought if they saw me now?" the actual presence of their parents (or of other people more generally) is not required. At the other end of the spectrum of values are individual preferences in matters of taste, leisure, and consumption. Those who grow up with a given style of cooking or a given range of sports activities typically learn to enjoy them, and to engage in them because they enjoy them, without any pressure from others.

In other words, I am stipulating a distinction between imitation and learning on the hand and sanctioning by disapproval on the other as two culture-sustaining mechanisms. The former applies to values, the latter to social norms. In practice, the distinction is often blurred. Deviation from values may well trigger disapproval. Yet the fact that others may in fact disapprove of deviations doesn't imply that their disapproval is what keeps deviations from occurring. One might just as well argue that because a ball rolling down a path between two walls *would be* prevented by the walls from leaving the path were it to deviate from its course, those walls actually *do* keep it on the path. As in the case of coordination equilibria discussed above, social norms may constitute a backup system that provides a reason for sticking to the relevant behavior when the usual motivation, for some reason, fails to do its work. In fact, some behaviors may have multiple supports. If my self-interest is not sufficient to make me obey the rules of traffic, moral respect for the law may help me do it. And if that isn't sufficient either, my fear of social disapproval may clinch the matter.

Beliefs

Human groups may also differ because they have different systems of beliefs. I do not have in mind norm-related beliefs, such as beliefs about the willingness of other people to sanction deviations from a social norm. These beliefs, although factual, I classify as part of the normative aspect of culture. Nor do I refer to beliefs about the likelihood that other people will conform to a specific coordination equilibrium.[7] Rather, I have in mind beliefs about causality, notably those from which one can infer ends-means relations. Two groups might have the same values, norms, and coordination equilibria and yet show different behavioral patterns because of different beliefs about which means are likely to be efficient to realize specific (shared) ends. Conversely, different values or norms might generate the same behavior if the normative differences are offset by cognitive differences.

As an illustration of these relations among values, beliefs, and behavior, consider the debates over unicameralism versus bicameralism in the French Assemblée Constituante of 1789.[8] Very broadly speaking, the assembly contained three groups. The reactionary right wanted to set the clock back to absolute monarchy, the moderate center wanted a constitutional monarchy with strong checks on parliament, and the left wanted a constitutional monarchy with fewer and weaker checks on parliament. On the issue of bicameralism, the positions were as shown in table 4.1.

For an example closer to the topics of this book, consider contemporary attitudes toward smoking, more specifically, other people's smoking. For some, the only reason that can justify a ban on smoking in public is that the practice imposes physical harm on others. For others, one may legitimately ban public smoking to help smokers who are trying to quit, the idea being that the sight of others who smoke will trigger cue-dependent relapse. The two groups arrive at the same conclusion, but from different normative and factual premises. The first group holds the normative premise that one may legitimately prevent people from imposing physical harm on others and the factual premise that passive smoking is a serious health risk. The second group holds the normative premise that one may legitimately impose sacrifices on some individuals in order to help others to overcome their weakness of will and the factual premise that the sight of others smoking may trigger relapse. The more general "antismoking culture" characteristic of some segments of Western societies also owes much, of course, to social norms against smoking as a *self*-destructive behavior.

Table 4.1
Positions on bicameralism in the French Assemblée Constituante of 1789

	Value priority	Belief	Behavior
Reactionaries	To destabilize the regime.	Bicameralism will stabilize the regime.	Vote for unicameralism.
Moderates	To stabilize the regime.	Bicameralism will stabilize the regime.	Vote for bicameralism.
Radicals	To stabilize the regime.	Bicameralism will destabilize the regime.	Vote for unicameralism.

Concepts

A final aspect of culture is the stock of concepts available to the members of a group. This is not a separate component of culture but rather is implicit in many of the components discussed above. For a phenomenon to be the object of a belief, a social norm, or a value assessment, the concept of that phenomenon must first exist. Conversely, a group that lacks a certain concept does not allow its members to entertain cognitive or normative attitudes toward the corresponding phenomenon. A society that lacks our concept of chance, for instance, does not allow for certain kinds of excuses and explanations. For the ancient Greeks, there was no such thing as an "innocent accident"; military commanders were held responsible for defeats that we would ascribe to the vagaries of the weather.[9] In seventeenth-century England, "any fortunate coincidence could be recognized as a 'providence' and any lucky escape might be seen as a 'deliverance': the casual visitor who arrived at the moment when some unhappy man was about to commit suicide; the horse which stumbled when its rider was on the way to make an unsatisfactory marriage; the sudden death which overtook some persecutor of God's people—such was the stuff of the anecdotes which the pious collected and recorded in their journals."[10]

Just as beliefs presuppose concepts, a concept may presuppose or embody a belief. When we talk about "the disease concept of madness," for instance, we presuppose a set of beliefs about a physiological basis for the disorder, its involuntary nature, the lack of responsibility for one's behavior, and so on. Initially, the disease concept of madness was an extension of the concept of disease to include mental as well as somatic disturbances. There was a concept of disease, a concept of madness, *and* a belief that the former is instantiated in the latter. Over time, the belief was gradually incorporated into the concept of madness itself. Although belief formation and concept formation are closely linked, at any given point in time one can distinguish between features of a phenomenon that belong to it by definition and features believed merely to characterize it. Cultural change can thus occur both by the emergence of novel beliefs about the relation between preexisting concepts and by changes in the concepts themselves.

A concept can also affect the reality it is supposed to capture. The widespread diffusion of psychoanalytic concepts such as "unconscious wish," "resistance," and "repression" has shaped people's thinking about themselves and about others. After Freud, it is less imperative to *argue* with opponents, since one has the option of dismissing their views as an expression of resistance to one's own. The explicit conceptualization of a phenomenon may also cause there to be more instances of it. Thus the element of truth in the "stigma theory of madness" is that when deviant behavior is conceptualized as mental illness, individuals who might otherwise have led functioning if perturbed lives are subjected to private ostracism and bureaucratic interference that transform what may have been no more than eccentricity into grounds for treatment and perhaps institutionalization. Although the core mental disorders exist independently of how we describe them, marginal cases can be affected by mere conceptualization.

Culture as Shared

I now come to the "important qualification" that I mentioned in the first sentence of section 4.1. It is that the mere fact of members of a group behaving in the same way, or having the same norms, values, and beliefs, does not by itself constitute a pattern of culture. In addition to these shared characteristics, I shall require, as Charles Taylor says in a different context, that "the sharing itself be shared."[11] I shall require, that is, that the members of the group are aware of the fact that others hold similar norms, values, and beliefs, or that they can be expected to behave in a similar manner. Whether or not one also makes it part of the definition that each member is aware that others are aware of this fact, etc., these higher-order beliefs can usually be assumed to obtain.

As Timur Kuran has shown, common knowledge of common norms, values, and beliefs cannot be taken for granted.[12] Under a variety of circumstances, people may have an incentive to keep their real norms, values and beliefs to themselves, and instead express norms, values, and beliefs that they do not hold. In some cases, these expressions are not taken seriously. In a "culture of hypocrisy" such as China during the Cultural Revolution or the former Soviet Union, everybody knows that nobody is sincere when they praise the regime or condemn its critics. In other cases, though, people may be led into error by taking what others say at face value. Writing about prerevolutionary France, Tocqueville asserts,

What with the loquacity of the opponents of Christianity and the silence of those who were still believers, there ensued a state of affairs that has often since been seen in France, not only as regards religion but also in quite different spheres of human behavior. Those who retained their belief in the Doctrines of the Church became afraid of being alone in their allegiance and, dreading isolation more than error, professed to share the sentiments of the majority. So what was still the opinion of only a part of the nation came to be regarded as the will of all and for this reason seemed irresistible even to those who had given it this false appearance.[13]

In the light of this and similar examples, we might ask whether the concept of culture sketched above ought to be revised. Instead of requiring both commonly held norms, values, and beliefs and the *knowledge* that they are shared, we might require merely the *belief* that they are shared, whether or not this actually is the case. The latter and weaker definition has the advantage of including important pathological cases, or "quasi cultures." It also fragilizes the concept, by allowing a culture to evaporate more or less instantly if someone points out that the emperor has no clothes on. This feature of the weak definition may be an advantage or a disadvantage, depending on the purpose of the analysis. Below I usually adopt the stronger definition.

Summary

I have proposed a conception of culture in terms of several interrelated components: coordination equilibria, shared social norms, shared values, shared beliefs, and shared concepts. The first of these is directly defined in terms of behavior. The others are also capable of inducing specific forms of behavior and owe much of their importance to this fact. I have not addressed the question of how cultures emerge and disappear, not because I think it unimportant, but because I find it too difficult. To my knowledge, the social sciences have not proposed any robust answer to this question. Functionalist claims to the effect that coordination equilibria or social norms arise when and because they would be socially useful tend to be speculative and unsupported by evidence. Claims by Marx and Tocqueville to the effect that various religious beliefs can be explained by the fact that they "reflect" the underlying social order are equally conjectural.[14] Although the history of science has established some general propositions about belief formation and concept formation, by the nature of the case it cannot enable us to predict new knowledge.

4.2 Culture and Emotion

The emotions are very closely linked to some of the aspects of culture that I have outlined. I shall mainly emphasize three aspects. (1) Emotions provide the main support of social norms. Although the emotions that sustain social norms seem to be universal, the behavior targeted by these norms varies from one group to another. (2) Not all cultures recognize or conceptualize the same emotions. Even if the emotions themselves are universal (as I conjecture), it does not follow that they are universally recognized. (3) When an emotion does belong to the conceptual repertoire of a culture, it can also become the target of prescriptive or proscriptive social norms, leading to either more or less frequent occurrences of the emotion than one would otherwise have observed.

Emotions as Supports of Social Norms

A social norm, as I shall use the concept here, has four features. First, it is a noninstrumental injunction to act or to refrain from acting. Norms target actions for their own sake, not because of their consequences. The norm "always wear black in strong sunshine," as do people in Mediterranean countries to maintain circulation of air between the clothes and the body, is an instrumental one. By contrast, the norm "always wear black at funerals" is noninstrumental. For reasons stated above, I do not count the avoidance of sanctions as a benefit that can be instrumentally promoted by following the norm.

Second, for a norm to be *social*, it has to be shared with other members of the relevant group, known to be shared, and so on. There exist noninstrumental norms that are purely private. A person living in a society that lacks norms of vengeance may nevertheless adopt the rule of getting even with anyone who has insulted or offended him, not in order to build a reputation that may be useful in future encounters but simply as a matter of personal principle. He may, for instance, follow the rule of not tipping taxi drivers whom he suspects of having taken a needlessly circuitous route. We can imagine most people adopting this rule, and yet it would not be a social norm unless it was known to be adopted by most people.

Third, social norms guide behavior by the sanctions imposed on those who violate them. Although many writers have argued that social norms amount *only* to a system of material sanctions,[15] I believe their view is misguided. For one thing, it is hard to see what motivation other people could have for sanctioning norm violators. Although failures to sanction may themselves be subject to sanctioning, this mechanism becomes increasingly implausible as we move away from the original norm violation.[16] For another, sanctions do not work by imposing material losses on their targets. When I refuse to deal with a person who has violated a social norm, he may suffer a financial loss. Far more important, however, he will see the sanction as a vehicle for the emotions of contempt or disgust, and suffer shame as a result. The material aspect of the sanction that matters is *how much it costs the sanctioner to penalize the target*, not how much it costs the target to be penalized. The more it costs me to refuse to deal with you, the stronger you will feel the contempt behind my refusal and the more acute will be your shame.

Fourth, social norms are thus also sustained by the emotion of shame, triggered by contempt as expressed through other people's sanctioning behavior. As we saw in section 2.3, contempt and shame have the same cognitive antecedent, namely the belief that the person toward whom the contempt is directed is a bad person. Although the immediate action tendency of shame is to hide or to disappear, or even to kill oneself, the emotion also affects behavior indirectly by inducing the individual to avoid situations that might trigger it.

It is almost impossible to exaggerate the painfulness of being exposed to the contempt of others. A. O. Lovejoy quotes Voltaire as saying, "To be an object of contempt to those with whom one lives is a thing that none has ever been, or ever will be, able to endure," Adam Smith as asserting, "Compared with the contempt of mankind, all other evils are easily supported," and John Adams to the effect that "The desire of esteem is as real a want of nature as hunger; and the neglect and contempt of the world as severe a pain as gout and stone."[17] In nineteenth-century Corsica, contempt for the person who failed to abide by the norms of vengeance was expressed by the *rimbecco*, "a deliberate reminder of the unfulfilled revenge. It could take the form of a song, a remark, a gesture or a look, and could be delivered by relatives, neighbours or strangers, men or women. It was a direct accusation of cowardice and dereliction."[18]

The life of the individual who is exposed every day to the *rimbecco* is hell. . . . "Whoever hesitates to revenge himself," said Gregorovius in 1854, "is the target of the whisperings of his relatives and the insults of strangers, who reproach him publicly for his cowardice." . . . "In Corsica, the man who has not avenged his father, an assassinated relative or a deceived daughter *can no longer appear in public*. Nobody speaks to him; he has to remain silent. If he raises his voice to emit an opinion, people will say to him: avenge yourself first, and then you can state your point of view." The *rimbecco* can occur at any moment and under any guise. It does not even need to express itself in words: an ironical smile, a contemptuous turning away of the head, a certain condescending look— there are a thousand small insults which at all times of the day remind the unhappy victim of how much he has fallen in the esteem of his compatriots.[19]

When contempt is expressed so publicly and so dramatically, nobody can fail to know the fate that awaits them if they violate the norm. Anticipated shame can then be a very effective regulator of behavior. In groups where contempt is less institutionalized, people may not be able to fully anticipate the strength of the shame they will incur.

To my knowledge, social norms and the emotions of contempt and shame that sustain them exist in all human groups. By contrast, the actions prescribed or proscribed by the norms vary enormously across groups. Thus norms of vengeance may be contrasted with the norm of turning the other cheek, and norms against marrying early with norms against marrying late. Sexual behavior proscribed within one group may be fully accepted in another. The norm against incest, although virtually universal, differs dramatically in scope across groups. In one group of workers, contempt may be directed against those who work too little; in another, against those who work too much; and in some groups the two norms may coexist.

Such examples could be multiplied indefinitely. What they show is not that the emotions themselves are subject to cultural variation but that certain (invariant) emotions sustain the norms that sustain variations in behavior. In addition, variation in behavior can be sustained by differences in values. These, however, are not in turn sustained by emotions. Although the violation of a moral or religious value tends to trigger anger in observers and guilt in the subject, the reason that people stick to their values is not that they anticipate these reactions. Nor are subjective values—preferences and tastes—supported by emotions.

Emotions as the Object of Cognition

To address the question of cultural variation in the emotions themselves, I need to consider two aspects of the relation between emotion and cognition that I have neglected so far. In section 2.3, I argued that (1) complex human emotions are caused by cognition. In addition, (2) emotion may be the object of cognition, and (3) cognition may be the effect of emotion. It will turn out that in many important cases, all three relations obtain simultaneously and interact with each other.

As noted in section 2.3, an individual may be in the grip of an emotion and not be aware of it. We have all heard, and many of us uttered, the angry utterance "I am not angry!" Similarly, a person may be in love and not be aware of it; be envious of another's achievement and not be aware of it; and so on. Other people may have no difficulty in detecting the emotion, but the person concerned remains unaware of it. In some cases the unawareness may be motivated or self-deceptive.[20] We may contrast, for instance, Mme. de Rênal's genuine lack of awareness of her love for Julien Sorel in *Le rouge et le noir* with the self-deceptive unawareness of the

Princesse de Clèves when, in the novel of the same name, she refuses to acknowledge her love for the Duc de Nemours.

In many cases, the individual concerned is capable of becoming aware of the emotion. (When unawareness is motivated, the individual must in fact already recognize the emotion at some level, in order to suppress it.) Once the emotion becomes the object of cognition, the latter may in turn trigger new emotions, or metaemotions. A person who consciously acknowledges love for an illicit partner may come to feel guilt or shame for the emotion. The relation between emotions and social norms is in fact a two-way street. Emotions regulate social norms but can also be the target of norms. I return to this issue below.

In other cases, the individual is prevented by idiosyncratic character traits from becoming aware of what he feels. Thus Michael Lewis reports, "I had a patient named John who received the news that a very dear aunt had died. At first, he reported experiencing great sadness at the loss. But then his sadness seemed to dissipate. Several weeks later, he felt agitated and experienced some trouble eating and sleeping. When I asked John how he felt, he replied that he felt tired. When I asked him whether he was depressed, he said that he did not feel depressed."[21] Lewis suggests two mechanisms that might explain why John did not acknowledge the fact that he was depressed: self-deception (see above) and socialization. The latter is spelled out as follows. "As a child, John may have exhibited certain behaviors in situations of loss. When he did, his parents informed him that these behaviors meant that he was tired, not sad. In other words, past experience may be capable of shaping people's self-awareness about an emotion, even to the extent of producing an awareness that is idiosyncratic in relation to the actual emotional state."[22]

In still other cases, the obstacle to awareness is cultural rather than personal. Thus Robert Levy argues that in Tahiti the misperception of depression as mere fatigue is the rule rather than an idiosyncratic exception. When a Tahitian, "feeling strange after being separated from his *vahine*, interprets his feelings as illness and in so doing accepts a pervasive cultural pattern of playing down feelings of loss, it is evident that in some way and at some level he must know that he has suffered a significant loss. That is why his separation from his *vahine* made him feel sick or strange in the first place. That is, one 'feels' considerably more than cultural forms may make consciously accessible."[23] In this case an observer might be able to identify many of the characteristic signs of emotion: unbidden occurrence, sudden onset, cognitive antecedent, arousal, valence, action tendency, and physiological expressions. A feature conspicuously lacking is the presence of an intentional object. Feelings of fatigue are not the kind of mental state that *can* have an intentional object.

The emotion of depression does not belong to the conceptual repertoire of the Tahitians. Similarly, Bernard Williams has argued that the emotion of guilt did not belong to the repertoire of the ancient Greeks; Patricia Spacks that the emotion of boredom, conceptualized as an involuntary mental state rather than as a reprehensible sin, did not exist until fairly recently; and C. S. Lewis that the emotion of romantic love did not arise until the European Middle Ages.[24] Williams and Spacks also make the point (overlooked by Lewis) that the mental states themselves and their attendant expressions can exist even if there is no concept that captures them. They make the further crucial observation that when the emotion *is* conceptualized, it is also changed.[25] When a person has the conceptual wherewithal to say to himself, "God, I'm bored!" the state of boredom will typically become more acute and efforts to alleviate it more intense.

These examples show that an emotion may exist at the behavioral and physiological level even when it is not conceptualized as such. In these cases we may say that the emotion exists as a *protoemotion*. When the emotion is conceptualized, we may say that it exists as a *proper emotion*. It is tempting to say that all the emotions that I enumerated in section 2.2 exist in all human groups, either as protoemotions or as proper emotions. One might even try to defend the stronger thesis that any emotion that exists as a proper emotion in some group will be found in all groups, either as a protoemotion or as a proper emotion. In that case, cultural variation would exist only at the level of conceptualization, not in the emotions themselves. Because of my lack of competence in the field of the anthropology of the emotions, I remain agnostic with respect to either thesis. Although some claims that certain emotions are nonuniversal may rest on a confusion between the existence of an emotion and its presence in conceptualized form, I am in no position to assert that this fallacy underlies all claims of this kind.

Emotions as the Object of Social Norms

When an emotion exists as a proper emotion, that is, as part of the conscious cultural repertoire of a group, the awareness can affect how the emotion is experienced as well as its role in social interaction. This effect may come about in several ways. (1) The concept may embody beliefs about the nature of the phenomenon. Once a state is conceptualized as depression, the person may think of it as long-lasting and unamenable to intervention, and may sink more deeply into the state. (2) The concept may change expectations about other people. Once a person can label his emotional state as love, he does not simply want to be with the other person: he wants to be loved in return. (3) A proper emotion can become subject to social norms, which may change how it is experienced. Arlie Hochschild gives the example of a feminist mother who feels guilty about leaving her child in day care and feels ashamed of her guilt. (4) An emotional state may also be viewed as violating a moral value. In a contrasting example from Hochschild, a traditionalist mother may think she feels too little guilt about leaving her child in day care and may in fact feel guilty about her lack of guilt.[26] In each of the last two cases the mothers would have to possess the concept of guilt, since otherwise the presence or absence of that emotion could not trigger the metaemotions of shame or guilt.

Yet these last cases also present a puzzle: how can emotion (or the lack of emotion) be subject to social norms or moral values? From the premises (i) that guilt attaches to voluntary action and (ii) that the emotions are involuntary, it follows that emotions should not trigger guilt. But they do. From the premises (iii) that shame is induced by the disapproving stare of others and (iv) that the emotions are unobservable, it follows that emotions should not trigger shame. But they do. One solution to these puzzles is to assume that the agent irrationally denies (ii) or (iv).[27] Another is to assume that the agent accepts (ii) and (iv) but irrationally feels guilt or shame nonetheless. Whatever the correct answer or answers to the puzzles, there is no doubt that emotional reactions or lack of reaction may trigger shame or guilt. Some people feel guilty for not grieving when a close relative dies, for not being happy on the day of their wedding, or for being in love with the wrong person (the Princesse de Clèves). Others feel ashamed of being afraid, of being envious, or of being in love with the wrong person (Mathilde de la Mole in *Le rouge et le noir*).

A less paradoxical phenomenon is that social norms can be directed at the *expression* of occurrent emotions. Although these expressions are largely involuntary, they can to some extent be suppressed or faked. Moreover, imperfect suppression or faking may be all that the social norm requires. For one thing, most people are not very good at noticing what an expert may perceive as telltale signs of suppression or faking.[28] For another, the norm may simply require a stylized performance of an emotion rather than one that has to be perceived as genuine. The grave look that is appropriate at funerals is not intended to communicate any specific mental state. Paid mourners are not paid to feel genuine grief (although they may well come to do so as a result of feedback from expression to the emotion itself).

Another, less paradoxical phenomenon is that people

may have emotional reactions triggered by beliefs about their emotional *dispositions*.[29] A person may be depressed by his inability to love, ashamed at his irascibility, angry at his tendency to feel irrational guilt, and so on. Cases of this kind seem to be less puzzling than those that involve guilt or shame for occurrent emotions. According to a long-standing tradition in philosophy and psychotherapy, emotional dispositions, like other character traits, are under the control of the will. Once the disposition is acquired, its being triggered on a particular occasion may be involuntary, but its acquisition in the first place was not. Aristotle, for instance, asserts a two-stage theory of this kind: "To the unjust and to the self-indulgent man it was open at the beginning not to become men of this kind, and so they are such voluntarily; but now that they have become so it is not possible for them not to be so" (*Nichomachean Ethics* 1114a, 20). To the extent that the acquisition of a disposition was voluntary, it is not irrational to blame oneself for having it. Whether that extent is substantial or minimal is another issue, which I postpone until section 5.2. Here I shall only note that if dispositions are under the control of the will of the agent and subject to social norms, we would expect them to be subject to cultural variation.

Emotions As the Cause of Cognition

I shall now add a final link in the chain of mechanisms that may produce cultural variation in occurrent emotions. It turns on the capacity of emotion to modify and distort cognition. Figure 4.1 offers an example that in fact involves all three relations between emotion and

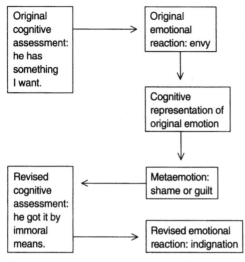

Figure 4.1
Three relations between cognition and emotion..

cognition. I assume here that the emotion of envy belongs to the repertoire of the group in question, that social norms or moral values stigmatize feelings of envy, and that on a given occasion the individual is aware that he is feeling envious. It follows that the individual will feel a metaemotion of shame or guilt. Let me focus on the emotion of shame, which is generally agreed to be more intensely unpleasant and have stronger motivational power than that of guilt.[30] The experience of envy and shame of envy may trigger various types of reactions. The individual might simply shrug his mental shoulders, think about something else, and forget the experience. Alternatively, he might defuse the emotion by the cognitive strategy of focusing on features that make the situation of the envied person less enviable. Looking at a rival, a woman might tell herself, "Yes, she is beautiful now, but think how miserable she will be when she loses her bloom." Finally, the envious person might use a more virulent cognitive strategy: rewriting the script to persuade oneself that the envied person obtained his possession in an illegitimate way and perhaps at the expense of the envious person. The man who fails to get a promotion he hoped for may tell himself that his rival got it through obsequious behavior and malicious talk. This new way of looking at the situation triggers the intoxicating feeling of righteous indignation, which can be indulged in freely without any tinge of shame. The new emotion may also induce behavior, such as attempts to redress the injustice or to punish the undeserving rival.

The ability of emotion to shape cognition is, of course, a very general phenomenon. In the more specific mechanism described in figure 4.1, an emotionally modified cognition is capable of modifying emotion. Whether the mechanism is triggered depends both on the strength of the original emotion and on the strength of the meta-emotion. In the case of envy, the frequency and intensity with which it occurs may vary across groups. Small towns and villages seem to be breeding grounds for envy, whereas it may occur less frequently in groups characterized by greater anonymity and social mobility. Although envy is usually an object of disapproval, the condemnation can be stronger in some groups than in others. Contemporary Western societies are probably at one extreme on this scale. One rarely justifies aggressive behavior by saying "He's getting too big for his shoes" or "Who does he take himself for?" A more elaborate story is usually needed. In other societies the story can be very thin indeed. Hence we would expect a great deal of envy whenever the conditions for the emotion to arise are present without there being strong norms against it. Conversely, envy would be rare either when it is repressed by strong norms or when the conditions that favor it are absent.

Justifying the Emotions

A comparison between the ancient Greeks and modern Western societies may provide further insight into the relation between emotions and the norms condemning them. Among the ancient Greeks, the term of praise *kalos* was used to denote beauty as well as other forms of excellence; conversely, its antonym *aishkros* could mean "shameful" as well as "ugly."[31] For them, "wealth and the achievements made possible by wealth [were] *kalos*, while poverty and the limitations which it imposes [were] *aishkros*. This is one reason why *aishkros* was sometimes applied to behavior which was not the fault of the agent."[32] Joshua Ober cites a reference to a law "that forbade anyone to reproach any Athenian, male or female, with working in the agora,"[33] which presupposes both a tendency to disapprove of such work and a tendency to disapprove of the disapproval. In our society, the latter is sufficient to neutralize the former, either because the latter is very strong or because the former is very weak. Among the Greeks, the relative strength of the two tendencies was such that a law was needed.

For us as well as for the Greeks, observable achievements and appearances are grounds for approval and pride. There is a difference, however, in the extent to which *failure* to meet standards of achievement and appearance provide grounds for blame and shame. In our society we do not blame people for what is outside their control. When we express disapproval of, and induce shame in, the obese and the unemployed, it is usually when and because we believe they could have been otherwise had they wanted to and tried hard enough. On the other hand, we do not express disapproval of the disfigured or the hardworking street vendor. The Greeks were more consistent. In their society the irrational contempt for the ugly or those born poor was matched by an equally irrational admiration of the beautiful or those born rich. This difference between the Greeks and ourselves arises because they *felt little shame in inducing shame* in others under circumstances in which we would be strongly censored for doing so.[34]

In this case too we may ask about the direction of causation between emotion and cognition. If citizens of modern societies believe that the obese or the unemployed have only themselves to blame for their condition, the belief may derive from our need to justify our contempt for them rather than from impartial consideration of the evidence. If we do not similarly blame the disfigured for their fate, one reason may be that it is harder to come up with a plausible story to justify a negative emotional reaction. If and when the concept of obesity becomes subsumed under that of involuntary disease, here too the lack of a plausible story may prevent us from giving in to our spontaneous emotional reactions.

This example suggests a second way in which concept formation can affect emotion. Earlier I argued that metaemotions exist only with respect to proper emotions, and not with respect to protoemotions. Here I have argued that lack of an appropriate conceptual category may prevent the metaemotion from triggering cognitive rewriting. We may again use envy to illustrate the mechanism. In addition to the transmutation of envy into righteous indignation illustrated in figure 4.1, we sometimes observe the transmutation of envy into *bitterness*, an emotion based on the belief that one's lack of fortune is undeserved.[35] Although the emotion of bitterness is less welcome than that of indignation (which is based on the belief that the other's fortune is undeserved), it is subjectively more acceptable than that of envy. Yet the transmutation of envy into bitterness depends on the ability to come up with a credible excuse. In our society, one can plausibly tell oneself and others a story that excuses the lack of fortune with a physical disability, but one cannot use a lazy disposition as an excuse.[36] If and when genes for laziness are identified, we might also modify our concept of laziness and our notion of when the emotion of bitterness is appropriate. For all sorts of reasons, that's unlikely to happen, yet the thought experiment may still be useful.

Summary

I have tried to isolate some strands in the dense network of relations between emotion and culture. The most important involve the dual relation between emotions and social norms. On the one hand, the emotions of shame and contempt sustain the social norms that prescribe and proscribe behavior within a specific group. On the other hand, occurrent emotions, emotional expressions, and emotional dispositions are themselves subject to social norms. Another important strand involves relations between emotion and cognition. An emotion cannot be the target of a social norm unless it is part of the conceptual repertoire of the group in question. Also, causal beliefs may constrain our ability to justify our emotions. I have not addressed the question of whether emotions are universal, not because I think it is unimportant, but because I do not know the answer. I have argued, however, that even if the concept of a given emotion is not found in a given group, we cannot infer that the members do not experience it, any more than the lack of the concept of agency in a society would allow us to infer that its members do not act.

4.3   Culture and Addiction

Emotions are universal, at least in the minimal sense that all human beings are subject to some emotions. Addiction, by contrast, is not a universal phenomenon. Although Norman Zinberg states, "All known societies (with the possible exception of earlier Eskimo cultures) have used intoxicants for recreational purposes,"[37] this is not a claim about the near-universal nature of *addiction*. Substances with an addictive potential can be and often are consumed nonaddictively. In some societies, nonaddictive use appears in fact to be the main or even the only form of consumption. In their classic study *Drunken Comportment* (1969), Craig MacAndrew and Robert Edgerton showed that in many societies, alcohol use has been regulated so that people could get drunk occasionally without turning into drunkards.

In still other societies, consumption is what *we* would call addictive, although members of the society in question do not think of it in that way. These societies exhibit what we may call—on an analogy with emotion—*pro-toaddiction*. Only in a few societies do we find *proper addiction*, that is, both the fact and the concept of addiction. Also, in societies that exhibit (what we call) addiction, the substances that sustain it differ greatly. The explanation of these variations lies in geography as well as in culture. People can get addicted to nicotine, cannabis, cocaine, or opium only if the relevant plants are available. Although alcoholic beverages can be made under a large variety of natural conditions, spontaneous fermentation of sugar-containing products cannot occur everywhere. In the modern world, these geographical factors have obviously lost much of their importance.

In the following, I shall focus on the variation in addictive behavior—initiation, acceleration, maintenance, and relapse—that can be explained in the terms outlined in section 4.1 above: coordination equilibria, social norms, values, and cognition (beliefs and concept formation). My aim is not to produce a theory of addiction in its relation to culture but only to point out some mechanisms that can help explaining cross-cultural variations in consumption that are not explicable in terms of geography. I assume throughout that the physiology of addiction is the same in all groups. Although there are inborn racial variations in the rate at which different addictive substances are metabolized, they seem to play a relatively marginal role in explaining addiction.[38] In any case, even if such differences exist, they cannot explain variations over time within a given population.[39]

Coordination Equilibria

Many forms of addictive substances are consumed in social isolation, especially at advanced stages. The solitary drinker and the heroin-addicted doctor hide their addiction from the world and have no desire to consume in the company of others. But many acts of consumption also occur in public. They take place in the presence of other consumers and are causally linked to others' consumption. The causal link can go in either direction. On the one hand, addicts may seek out fellow addicts to persuade themselves that their behavior is entirely normal. The alcoholic may "rationalize the need by assertions that he or she drinks no more than his or her friends. Accordingly, alcoholics tend to spend their time with other drinkers."[40] On the other hand, people who might otherwise not have consumed may be induced to do so by the presence of fellow consumers.

There are in fact several mechanisms by which one person's consumption of an addictive drug may increase the likelihood of another's consumption. The sight of another person smoking may trigger the desire for a cigarette (cue-dependent craving). As noted above, this effect is sometimes cited as an argument for a ban on smoking in public. In a different mechanism, modeled by Karl O. Moene, the presence of other consumers enters directly into the utility function. Although the model seems especially plausible for alcohol consumption, it may illuminate the use of other addictive substances as well. Let D indicate consumption, and let N indicate abstention.

The pleasure of consumption is represented by an individual utility function, $v = v(x, y)$, where x indicates the person's own choice and y what the others choose. The temptation to drink or to take drugs is assumed to be social in character. Thus when the others drink the person prefers to drink as well, and when the others do not drink the person also prefers to abstain. Formally,

$$v(D, D) > v(N, D),$$ (a.1)

$$v(N, N) > v(D, N),$$ (a.2)

which simply state that the individual does not like to deviate from what the others do. In addition, within a group of similar individuals a deviant behavior is assumed to impose a negative externality on the others. All else being equal, drinkers would rather interact with another drinker than with a non-drinker; and persons who like not to drink would rather like to interact with other non-drinkers than with drinkers. Stated formally, this can be expressed as

$$v(D, D) > v(D, N),$$ (a.3)

$$v(N, N) > v(N, D).$$ (a.4)

The preferences indicated by (a.1)–(a.4) are conformist in two ways. On the one hand (a.1) and (a.2) state that people like to imitate what others do. On the other hand, (a.3) and (a.4) state that people would like others to imitate their behavior.[41]

Moene shows that if potential drug consumers have conformist preferences of this kind, accidents of history can determine whether a society ends up in a high-use equilibrium or a low-use equilibrium. Beliefs and social norms are irrelevant for the outcome. Although conformism can also result from social pressure, Moene's model does not rely on sanctions imposed on deviants. As I argued in section 4.1, however, the two varieties of conformism are likely to coexist. A person who, by not drinking, makes others feel bad may easily become the target of their scorn. Thus a person who ventures into a bar is exposed to a triple pressure. If he has drunk heavily in the past, drink may be triggered by watching others drink (cue dependence). In addition, his behavior may be shaped by his desire to do what others do (preference-induced conformism) and by others taunting him to drink (norm-induced conformism). Thus even when a high-use coordination equilibrium *emerges* by the kind of conformism Moene describes, it may be *sustained* by several other mechanisms.

For all these reasons, it is often recommended that people who want to stop drinking or smoking avoid places where these activities go on.[42] As Moene shows, however, staying away from others will have costs, especially if a high fraction of the population engages in the activity. Some would-be quitters may be motivated to bear the costs, others may not. One can easily imagine cases in which no single individual is willing to bear the costs in isolation, yet coordinated behavior by all would-be quitters would reduce the costs sufficiently for all of them to be willing to bear them. Here the government may come to their assistance. "Polls over the past twenty years have consistently shown majority support among smokers for [restrictions on public smoking]. Many smokers view limitations on smoking as a way to help them quit, or at least reduce their consumption, and many also understand the need to control tobacco smoke pollution for the sake of others."[43]

Social Norms

Social norms explain a great deal of cross-cultural variation in the consumption of addictive substances, as is especially well brought out by considering variations in the use of alcohol.[44] In the following, I focus on alcohol, although I shall occasionally touch on other substances and behaviors as well.

In almost all known societies throughout history, people have used beer, wine, or liquor for nutritional, medical, ritual, and recreational purposes—or just to get drunk. Moreover, the use of these beverages is embedded in a very dense network of social norms and sanctions. There is enormous variety in drinking behavior and drinking norms across cultures, at least with regard to moderate drinking. Alcoholics, by contrast, seem to be similar everywhere. "With the development of drunkenness and alcoholism in subpopulations, we observe the increase of psychic degradation and asocial behavior, and the loss of originality of alcohol customs and alcohol culture."[45]

For simplicity, we may distinguish three levels of alcohol consumption: none (abstinence), moderate, and heavy. On any given occasion, heavy drinking may have undesirable consequences of various kinds, such as traffic accidents caused by drunk driving or violent behavior due to the disinhibiting effects of alcohol. Sustained heavy drinking over time has a different range of undesirable consequences. Whereas some of the medical harms caused by regular heavy use take a long time to develop and may well go unnoticed altogether (see below), others emerge more rapidly and are clearly visible. A person may drink so heavily that he is unable to keep his job, or his family life may go to pieces because of his heavy drinking.

If social norms were invariably utilitarian (section 4.1), we might expect them to be directed against heavy drinking that is perceived to have harmful short-term or long-term consequences for the drinking individual or for others. There are indeed many norms of this kind. Some of them enjoin total abstinence. To my knowledge, these norms are always linked to religion.[46] Islam and certain Protestant sects, for instance, have absolute bans on alcohol. Secular norms, by contrast, often enjoin drinking in moderation. The Italian norm "Never drink between meals" has the dual effect of limiting total consumption and of reducing the rate of absorption of alcohol into the body, thus buffering the short-term effect on the body. In Iceland, there are norms against drinking in the presence of the children and against drinking on fishing trips. Again, the norms have a dual function. In addition to reducing total consumption, they prevent undesirable effects on children, and they prevent work accidents.

Scandinavian countries more generally are governed by the following principles: "Drinking and working are kept strictly separate; drinking is still not integrated with everyday meals; and the main normative division tends to be one between non-drinking situations and situations where not only drinking but intoxication as well is culturally accepted."[47] In these countries, there are also strong norms against drunken driving. Many countries condemn solitary drinking in private. According to Dwight Heath, "The solitary drinker, so dominant an image in relation to alcohol in the United States, is virtually unknown in other countries."[48] Other countries condemn solitary drinking in public. Thus in Poland, "a woman who drinks alone in public may be regarded as a prostitute."[49]

Further norms regulate consumption of alcohol by providing narrow definitions of socially appropriate occasions for heavy drinking. MacAndrew and Edgerton give many examples to show how alcohol consumption and its effects may be regulated and limited by social norms:

In each of these societies the state of drunkenness is a state of societally sanctioned freedom from the otherwise enforceable demands that person comply with the conventional proprieties. For a while—but just for a while—the rules (or, more accurately, *some* of the rules) are set aside, and the drunkard finds himself, if not beyond good and evil, at least partially removed from the accountability nexus in which he normally takes a part. In a word, drunkenness in these societies takes on the flavor of "*time out*" from many of the otherwise imperative demands of everyday life.[50]

In some societies, there are norms that condemn heavy drinking on any occasion. Among Jews, especially in the Diaspora, drunkenness is often seen as a feature of Gentiles. Similarly, "Spaniards hold a cultural prejudice against intoxication, drunkenness being a sort of ethnic boundary attributed to outsiders. In fact, Spaniards derived a sense of superiority over northern Europeans and over the natives they ruled in their colonies because of their 'civilized' attitude toward drinking. In colonial Mexico, . . . local Spanish officials saw excessive drinking as a custom that supported their view of Mexicans as 'perpetual minors,' incapable of conforming to Spanish standards of moderation."[51] In Italy there is also a strong opprobrium attached to being drunk in public. The reason lies not so much in the harmful consequences of heavy drinking as in the fact that it reveals a deplorable lack of self-control. In traditional Catholic societies, excessive drinking and excessive eating were both condemned as manifesting lack of self-control (the sin of gluttony).[52]

Alcohol-related norms are not, however, always utilitarian. There are norms that condemn abstinence, as well as norms that enjoin people to drink heavily. Among the Mapuche Indians of Chile, drinking alone is criticized, and so is abstinence; such behavior is seen as showing lack of trust. Traditional French culture condemns both the teetotaler and the drunkard. In Italy, distrust of abstainers is expressed in a proverb, "May God protect me from those who do not drink." In the American colonial period, abstainers were often suspect (but drinking problems were infrequent). In youth subcultures of many countries, abstainers are subject to heavy pressure and ridiculing. Conversely, there are also many societies in which heavy drinking is socially prescribed. In Mexico and Nigeria, the macho qualities shown in the ability to drink heavily are much admired. In prerevolutionary Russia, excessive drinking was obligatory in the subculture of young officers. Among the Polish gentry, "drinking was a manifestation of an idle lifestyle and wealth. Heavy drinking seemed to be not only a right but almost a duty of a nobleman. A host used to urge his guests to drink heavily and felt offended if they refused. . . . Traces of these customs can be found in popular songs and sayings. Even today, Poles sing while drinking: 'And who will not drink to the bottom of the glass should be beaten with two sticks.'. . . In the 1700s, special wine cups without a foot were invented, to force a guest to drink a full cup in one gulp."[53]

When abstinence is condemned or when heavy drinking is socially mandatory, would-be abstainers may have to resort to subterfuge. In Sweden, "A common question is 'Do you want sherry, or are you driving?' It is so accepted that abstaining alcoholics often say they are driving because this relieves them of the social pressure that otherwise would certainly be exerted by the host to convince the guest to have a drink."[54] The norm of drinking can only be offset by another norm (against drunk driving). Similarly, it has been argued that conversions to Protestantism "provide an alternative for some Latin Americans who want to opt out of the costly and time-consuming civil-religious hierarchy of community governance in which even secular rituals often involve heavy drinking and drunkenness."[55] Again, the norm of drinking can be overridden only by another norm, which in this case has the backing of religion.

These are cases of the strategic use of norms. Conversely, people can behave strategically to get around the norms. Thus "some ancient Chinese considered alcohol itself to be sacred, and drank it only in sacrificial ceremonies; eventually, they would sacrifice whenever they wanted to drink."[56] In Spain, "at certain hours, not to drink on an empty stomach is a tacit cultural proscription, and food, even a morsel, will be included with the drinking."[57] In both cases, we observe a reverse of the original causal link: rather than drinking when they are doing x, people do x whenever they want to have a drink. People who abide by the social norm of not drinking before dinner may find themselves moving dinner forward so as to drink more and still be able to tell themselves (and others) that the norm is respected. Although such strategies do not render the norms entirely ineffective, they can undermine them.

Moderate drinking reflects a delicate balance between the desire for alcohol and the social norms that keep it within bounds. Since behavior is more easily learned and imitated than norms, one might expect excessive drinking when a drinking and a nondrinking culture meet. The excessive drinking by natives in Colonial Mexico (see above), may be due to this fact. The same mechanism applies to Israeli Arabs: "Islam prohibits alcohol consumption; the Jewish religion does not, but advocates moderation and warns against intoxication. These differences may explain why the incidence of daily drinking is higher among Arab men than Jewish men. The Arab who consumers alcoholic beverages separates himself from his religion and culture, and loses his social-religious support. . . . *He does not know how to drink and knows little about the nature of alcohol*. These factors can contribute to his excessive drinking."[58] The mechanism may also operate across generations. Thus according to a 1984 survey in Poland, "in 40% of the families, parents did not talk about alcohol; in only 20% were positive norms concerning drinking presented. . . . In such a situation, most youngsters experiment with alcohol on their own. . . . The adult pattern is sometimes imitated at the behavioral level but *lacks the complete normative context*. The lack of parental impact on socialization about alcohol leaves the children open to the influence of popular culture, which often emphasizes 'wet' patterns."[59]

A final comment on alcohol-related norms concerns their possibly counterproductive effects. Parental injunctions against drinking may have the opposite effect of the intended one, for one or several of the following four reasons. First, of course, young people very generally tend to oppose their parents. In Sri Lanka, for instance, "for young men, abstinence carries the implication of being unwilling or unable to break away from parental authority."[60] Second, the norms often convey the message that drinking is part of the adult world to which the adolescent desperately wants to belong. Third, people may form a desire to possess something simply because they are told they cannot have it ("forbidden fruit") or conversely, block their desire for it because they are told to consume it. Jack Brehm has investigated this phenomenon under the heading of "reactance."[61] Fourth, deliberate attempts to induce shame in others often induce anger and protest behavior rather than shame and avoidance behavior.[62] Shame is the correlate of spontaneous expressions of contempt, not of deliberate shaming behavior.

These are cases in which norms against drug taking induce drug taking in nonusers. Antidrug norms and values can also sustain the behavior at more advanced stages. Many who are subject to chemical or behavioral addictions incur strong feelings of shame (due to the perceived violation of a social norm) or guilt (due to a perceived violation of a moral norm). The need to blot out the awareness that one is making a mess of one's life can then be an important factor sustaining the behavior. The mechanism plays a role in sustaining not only alcoholism,[63] but also overeating,[64] compulsive shopping,[65] and compulsive gambling,[66] but not, it seems, in maintaining smoking behavior or heroin and cocaine abuse. Yet a similar mechanism has been identified as important in nicotine *relapse*. In the face of guilt induced by abstinence violation, "the individual is likely to resort to an old and familiar coping response— smoking."[67]

Cognition

The role of beliefs and concept formation in addiction is very important. Many of the social norms cited above, for instance, are intertwined with various beliefs about the effects of consumption. Again, alcohol will be my primary example, although I shall also refer to other addictive substances.

The modern concept of alcohol, which includes beer, cider, wine, and liquor, has not existed in all societies. Even in societies where all these beverages were consumed, they are not necessarily conceptualized together as "alcohol." "For over 30 percent of Poles, an abstainer is a person who may consume beer or wine but does not drink vodka."[68] In French, *"l'alcool* refers to a chemical substance contained in liquids obtained by fermentation, including good wine, that may cause intoxication. *Les alcools* refers exclusively to the product of distillation, perceived as more chemical, more 'industrial', and less 'natural'."[69] More generally, for people in the Mediterranean countries, wine has traditionally been a nutrient with "intoxicating side effects."[70]

The use of alcoholic beverages may be linked to various beliefs about their effects. "In Nigeria, as in most African countries, alcohol is considered food, a necessary nutrient rich in vitamins, a stimulant, a disinfectant necessary to the body to fight against cold, fear, weariness and intrusive microbes. . . . Alcohol is justifiedly considered a nutrient because Nigerian palm wine is reported to contain 145 milligrams of ascorbic acid and 100 grams of vitamin C per serving."[71] In Italy too "wine is seen as nourishment. In the past, the nutritional aspects were particularly relevant in the alimentation of the lower classes, whose poor diet needed precisely those extra calories that wine could provide."[72] Alcohol has also been used for its superior hygienic properties. In the English Middle Ages, "alcoholic drinks were often safer to consume than water or milk, given the sanitary conditions of the time."[73] In contemporary rural Mexico, "good drinking water is less easily accessible than alcohol."[74] One may always ask, however, whether the nutritional aspects of alcohol identified by modern observers are perceived by the consumers. Alcohol might simply have "nutritional side effects" while being consumed for its intoxicating properties.

Alcohol use and alcoholism can be iatrogenic when beer, wine, or liquor are taken or prescribed for their (alleged) medicinal properties. "The amount of wine used for therapeutic purposes in the hospitals of pre-revolutionary Russia exceeded its consumption per capita in the healthy population. The problems of alcohol therapy were most dramatic in pediatric practice; it often was the doctor who gave children their first wine."[75] In Nigeria, "there is a general belief that alcohol can relieve stomach problems. . . . Specifically, it is generally believed that Guinness stout . . . can cure dysentery."[76] In France, well into the 1900s it was actually thought wine could be used to cure alcoholism.[77] In French "medical lore from the 1500s to the 1700s, getting drunk was treated as a means of purging the body."[78]

As these examples show, many beliefs about the benefits of alcohol are false or dubious. People have also formed various false beliefs about the *harmful* properties of alcohol and other substances. The great "absinthe scare" provides an example.[79] There is no scientific basis for believing that this drink, which remains forbidden in all European countries except Great Britain, has any damaging long-term effects over and above those caused by its ethanol content. According to Jean-Charles Sournia, "one blamed the absinthe so that one would not have to blame alcohol."[80] There are several other cases in which the perception of long-term damage has been overstated, even wildly exaggerated. Zinberg notes, "Although many controlled users feel that heroin can be used moderately, they regard it as more rapidly addicting than is warranted by the pharmacology of the drug. This attitude, of course, is understandable in view of the prevailing myths about heroin's power as well as the exposure of controlled users to addicts who have succumbed to the drug."[81]

For further examples, consider the Victorian writer who described the long-term effects of coffee as follows: "The sufferer is tremulous and loses his self-command; he is subject to fits of agitation and depression. He has a haggard appearance. As with other such agents, a renewed dose of the poison gives temporary relief, but at the cost of future misery." He describes the effects of tea in equally dramatic terms: "An hour or two after breakfast at which tea has been taken a grievous sinking feeling may seize upon the sufferer so that to speak is an effort. The speech may become weak and vague. By miseries such as these, the best years of life may be spoilt."[82] Many beliefs about short-term harms are equally unfounded. Thus MacAndrew and Edgerton document, on the one hand, that many modern writers argue that heavy drinking always causes disinhibition and loss of control, and on the other, that in many societies people do in fact drink heavily without any such consequences.[83]

Conversely, harmful drugs may be seen as harmless. Whereas the misperception of short-term harm is unlikely, long-term damage may well go unnoticed. In some cases, it may essentially be unnoticeable. Asking why the skilled clinicians of antiquity failed to notice the organic lesions caused by alcohol, Sournia answers that the failure was "linked to the average life span of people at the time, probably about forty years. Cirrhosis of the liver, lesions of the pancreas and alcohol-induced cancers take several decades of intoxication before they manifest themselves, and even though some persons may be affected at a younger age the number of clinical cases was probably too small to attract the attention of doctors."[84] In other cases, the causal link is finally uncovered, but only with some delay. Thus the rapid increase in lung cancers between 1920 and 1950 was initially imputed to pollution rather than to the true culprit, smoking.[85] These examples concern only organic damage. There is much less uncertainty or ignorance attached to the often disastrous long-term effect of alcohol, heroin abuse, or compulsive gambling on the addict's financial and social situation. The addict himself may deny or deceive himself about these effects, but observers are unlikely to do so.

A particularly important set of beliefs is the idea that a given substance is addictive. Once a behavioral pattern is conceptualized as an addiction, with the concomitant causal beliefs, it may change dramatically. An especially important belief is that addiction is, if not irresistible, at least very hard to resist, almost amounting to compulsive desire. (For the accuracy of this belief, see section 5.3 below.) Hence to the causal beliefs about the effects of drug taking on the addict's body and socioeconomic status, we must add causal beliefs about the effect of addiction on his *will*, more specifically, on his ability to quit. Two opposite beliefs about this effect may have the same impact on behavior. Some addicts use their (usually self-deceptive) belief that they can quit at any time as an excuse for not quitting. Others use their (equally self-deceptive) belief that they are unable to quit as an excuse for not quitting. The belief that one is addicted may reinforce the addiction by the mechanism of dissonance reduction. Often this mechanism will lead addicts either to deny that they are addicted or to deny that addiction is harmful.[86] While removing any motivation to change, these outcomes of dissonance reduction do not actually entrench the habit. In a third scenario, however,

counter-attitudinal behaviour (e.g., continued smoking in spite of acknowledgement of dangers to health) is not necessarily dissonance-arousing for individuals who see their behaviour as beyond their voluntary control (e.g., who say "I can't help myself"), or who selectively reduce their self-esteem (e.g., who say "I haven't the will-power"). In terms of this interpretation, "dissonant" smokers are not in a state of unresolved dissonance, once they label themselves as addicted. It may well be, then, that many smokers are motivated to see themselves as addicts. . . . As more smokers come to acknowledge the health risks of smoking, it is to be expected that they will become non-smokers or, more probably, that they will seek extra justification for their continued behaviour. To label smoking as an addiction provides such a justification, and hence, in our view, this is not a theme that should be incorporated in health education aimed at the established smoker.[87]

The concept of addiction, with the concomitant belief that the craving for the drug is nearly irresistible, is relatively modern. Before 1800, what we would call alcoholism was often perceived as a form of excessive behavior or gluttony.[88] It was a vice, not a condition. In reality, of course, heavy drinkers were addicted. They went to great lengths to find the next drink, looked for a drink the first thing in the morning, died from cirrhosis of the liver, and so on. They just didn't know they were addicted, any more than a young Tahitian whose girlfriend has left him knows that he is depressed. According to Harry Levine, the man responsible for the "discovery of addiction" was Benjamin Rush (1746–1813). "Rush's contribution to a new model of habitual drunkenness was fourfold: First, he identified the causal agent—spirituous liquors; second, he clearly described the drunkard's condition as loss of control over drinking behavior—as compulsive activity; third, he declared the condition to be a disease; and fourth, he prescribed total abstinence as the only way to cure the drunkard."[89] Levine adds,

> I do not mean to imply that some new style of drinking emerged which had not existed before and which was then labeled addiction. Colonial society could show as great a variety of styles of habitual drunkenness as the 19th century. Further, some alcoholism experts have read descriptions of drunkards as far back as ancient Greece and concluded that the drinking pattern they identify with alcoholism existed then. What was new in the 19th century was the legitimacy of a particular way of interpreting the experience and behavior of drunkards. In colonial society there may have been isolated individuals who felt "overwhelmed" by their desires for drink, but there was no socially legitimate vocabulary for organizing the experience and for talking about it; it remained an inchoate and extremely private experience. In

the 19th century the drunkard's experience was so familiar it became stereotyped.[90]

Prior to 1800, there existed what we may call *protoalcoholism* easily recognized by modern observers but not conceptualized as such by those who were subject to it and those around them. As in the analogous case of the emotions, when the phenomenon was conceptualized, it was also transformed. The idea that an alcohol addict can be cured only by total abstinence, for instance, entails a modification of the temporal pattern of drinking, with periods of abstinence alternating with bingeing. Once the would-be-reformed alcoholic has had one drink, the belief that it will inevitably bring about total relapse becomes self-fulfilling. Conversely, of course, that very same belief may also prevent him from taking the first drink. The belief can change behavior for the better or for the worse.[91]

More generally, attempts to quit an addiction presupposes the concept of addiction. As we shall see in section 5.3, addicts deploy a number of complicated strategies to remain abstinent or, sometimes, to consume in moderate amounts. They know, or believe, that they cannot simply decide to quit and then implement their decision. One might think that this belief is due to experience. Many addicts try the naive strategy of "just quitting" before they learn that more sophisticated techniques are needed. In my opinion, however, the belief is simply part of modern culture. What an addict learns in his failed attempts to quit is that he is what his culture labels an addict. To be addicted *is* to be unable to "just quit."

Other people too treat the modern alcoholic or nicotine addict differently from how they treated the drunkard or inveterate smoker of earlier times. The argument referred to above—that people should be prevented from smoking in public to remove cues from smokers who want to quit—presupposes that nicotine addiction is a disease of the will. More important, the modern concept of addiction may give rise to iatrogenic forms of the condition, as suggested by the following passages:

It has generally been assumed by alcoholism treatment personnel in most industrialized countries that the disease-labeling process and the alcoholic's concomitant acceptance of the "sick" role would facilitate treatment and potentiate the chances of rehabilitation. Some writers . . . , however, question the utility of indiscriminate application of the disease label, not only because it may not be appropriate for all varieties of alcohol-related problems, but also because *it may influence the very behavior it attempts to describe.* This could come about . . . by altering the cognitive expectancies held by alcoholics and by those in their immediate social environment, such that the drinker no longer is seen as responsible for his or her behavior. In this view, loss of control over drinking may result more from learned expectations than from physical predispositions, and chronic alcoholism more from a dependency role than from physiological dependence.

Another source of influence on alcoholics is the treatment process itself, since a major goal of treatment, especially in the U.S., is to convince the alcoholic of the validity of the disease concept, and to remove the personal stigma associated with the negative stereotype of the alcoholic.[92]

Summary

The interaction of social norms and causal beliefs about addictive substances explains a great deal of the variation in drug use across societies. Some of the norms are presumably directly induced by the beliefs. Norms against consuming in excess or on inappropriate occasions tend to target behavior believed to have adverse consequences. Other norms are more puzzling. Rather than steering the individual away from excess, they drive him away from abstention and may even direct him toward excess.

There is a core of truth in the idea that addiction is "all in the mind." To some extent, it doesn't matter whether a substance or behavioral pattern is actually addictive, as long as people believe it is. Also, many effects of addictive drugs are heavily shaped by expectations. In a typical two-by-two design, where subjects are either given the real drug (alcohol or nicotine) or a placebo, and are told either that they are given the real drug or given the placebo, some effects of the drug are more pronounced when they are given a placebo and told it's the drug than when they receive the drug and are told it's a placebo.

Yet these effects do not imply that culture is all-powerful in shaping addiction. Addiction is in the body as well as in the mind. The power of expectations to shape consumption experience is probably less than what was once believed. Many effects of "alcohol myopia" are not produced with placebos.[93] Smokers who are given cigarettes with lower nicotine content adjust their consumption upward after a while.[94] Social or moral norms may stop an addict from going on a binge of drinking, gambling, or crack using, but once a binge has begun, they are less effective in preventing him from going on until he collapses. Even though a proto-addiction may change dramatically once it is transformed into proper addiction, it can also have a powerful influence on behavior at the preconceptualized stage.

5   Choice, Emotion, and Addiction

5.1   The Concept of Choice

I shall discuss three levels of intentional action. First, there is "action without choice"—deliberate action that is insensitive to changes in the reward structure. Next, there is action based on "minimal choice"—deliberate action that can be modified by changes in the reward structure. Finally, there is the more complex idea of "rational choice"—deliberate action that stands in the right kind of relation to the desires, beliefs, and information sets of the agent. Although I shall argue that the concept of action without choice is a coherent one, it may be difficult to decide whether and when it is instantiated. By contrast, the concepts of minimal and rational choice are frequently instantiated.

Action without Choice

Ability to choose implies, minimally, sensitivity to expected rewards and punishments ("reward sensitivity" for short). Suppose that an agent has two feasible options, *a* and *b*, and does *a*. For that action to be the result of a choice, there must exist some modification of the rewards associated with a, b, or both that would have caused b to be performed. Thus if the agent does a even when he has information that would allow him to infer that the outcome will be disastrous compared to the consequences of b, we might question whether the action is the result of a choice. Imagine a person in a lifeboat whose horrible thirst causes him to drink sea water. Although he does not know that the sea water will cause him to die much more quickly than if he had abstained, we may stipulate that even if he had been in a position to know, he would have been unable to abstain. In that case, we might want to say that his desire was "irresistible" and that he "had no choice."

Note that when the castaway drinks, it is unambiguously a voluntary *action*—a deliberate bodily movement for the purpose of obtaining some goal. It is neither a piece of reflex behavior nor a mere event, as when a person falls asleep while driving. It is also more than what we might call a quasi action, as when a person finally gives in to an urge to urinate. Although a quasi action is preceded by some kind of mental assent, it is not an action in the sense defined above. The decision not to resist an urge of the body is not a movement of the body. (The urinating might also be a mere event if the person resisted until the very end.) Yet even though drinking the sea water is an action, it is at least arguable that it is the result not of a choice but of an "irresistible desire" to drink.

Gary Watson has recently discussed the claim that desires can be "irresistible," "compulsive," or "overpowering." He begins with an example of interpersonal compulsion: the bouncer who compels me to leave the room by literally picking me up and tossing me into the alley. He then goes on to ask, "Could I have a relation to (some of) my own desires that is sufficiently parallel to my relation to the bouncer's intentions to warrant non-metaphorical talk of compulsion?"[1] By and large, his answer is negative. Before I proceed to discuss his argument, I shall mention an objection he makes to the use of reward sensitivity as a criterion for choice. To combine my example and one of his examples, suppose that the only access to the sea water is through a pack of rats, to which the castaway has a phobic aversion. In that case, he might abstain from choosing the disastrous option. As Watson observes, the scenario "shows that no test of compulsion in terms of susceptibility to deterrent incentives will work without somehow ensuring that the motivation in the counterfactual scenario is not compulsive."[2] He does not discuss, however, how one might ensure the condition of noncompulsiveness. Below I suggest a test that will at least yield sufficient conditions.

Watson first observes that in paradigmatic cases of external compulsion, the agent is unable to resist a force or pressure even if he does his utmost to do so. Yet being unable to resist a strong desire is not analogous to being unable to resist the force of a boulder or that of a bursting bladder:

Unlike external obstacles (or internal pressures), motivational obstacles work in part not by defeating one's best efforts, but by leading one not to try. One's behavior is in an important sense voluntary. That is the crucial difference between the mass of the boulder and the motivational "force" of a desire. The mass of the boulder can overpower me by bypassing my will, whereas desire cannot. Being overpowered by the hunk of stone means that full unambivalent use of one's powers is insufficient to resist its force. Being defeated by a desire means that one's capacities to resist are not unambivalently deployed.[3]

He concludes that the apparently irresistible desires of addicts are best described by saying that they "have great difficulty in bringing reason effectively to bear on their choices in a certain region of deliberation, at least under some circumstances. This point places the emphasis on the corruption of practical reason rather than on the power of addictive desire. We are not so much overpowered by brute force as seduced."[4] I might add, following the discussion of addiction and cognitive dissonance in section 4.3 above, that the seduction operates in part through the belief that the desire *is* overpowering, so that any resistance will be fruitless.

I return to the case of addiction later in this chapter. Here I want to ask whether Watson's argument refutes the idea of an irresistible desire or, more precisely, the idea that some voluntary actions are reward-insensitive. I do not think it does (and it may not be intended to do so). The "corruption of practical reason" to which he refers may in fact have the effect of disabling the agent from paying attention to alternative actions and to long-term consequences of the action favored by the putative compulsive desire. The only thought in his mind is that an urgent discomfort will be relieved by taking a certain action, for example, by drinking sea water. If the effect of a desire or a craving is to make some options and consequences disappear from the cognitive horizon of the agent, there is a real sense in which he "has no choice." The agent is like a horse with blinkers, unable to detect, and hence to react to, dangers coming from outside his narrow field of attention.

I believe that this is a coherent conceptual account of nonchoice-based voluntary action. Whether and when it is instantiated is another matter. Later I discuss whether emotions or addictive cravings have the capacity to blot out awareness of options and consequences in this way. Although I have never been desperately thirsty, I imagine that the condition could well have this effect. Other forms of acute pain may induce a similar shrinking of the cognitive field.

One might, however, propose an alternative account in terms of a *temporarily enhanced rate of time discounting*. On this analysis, the agent would have full cognitive awareness of alternatives and consequences but simply attach less weight to them in his decisions. Rather than being totally insensitive to rewards, he would only be less sensitive to temporally distant rewards. If the bad consequences of the favored action were sufficiently magnified or moved forward in time, he would resist the desire to perform it.

In many cases, the analysis in terms of time discounting is certainly on target. I do not see how, in the present state of research, one could determine whether it is always adequate. For any apparently reward-insensitive action one could always argue that if the bad consequences were moved forwards in time so as to occur *very* shortly after the desired consequences, it would not be performed. To refute any counterexample to the time-discounting account, its defenders could always assert that the consequences simply have not been moved sufficiently close to the action. The issue could probably only be decided by neurophysiological evidence, which will not be forthcoming soon. To identify the neurophysiological substrate of complex beliefs about the consequences of behavior seems far beyond anything we can envisage today. Hence I propose that we characterize behavior as reward-insensitive if current experimental techniques cannot show the contrary.

Minimal Choice

As Watson argues, the fact that an action is sensitive to rewards does not in itself prove that it is the result of a deliberate choice among alternatives on the basis of their expected consequences. If the compulsive thirst of the castaway is conquered by an even stronger compulsive fear of rats, it would be misleading to say that he *chooses* not to drink. Yet there are, of course, many standard cases in which reward sensitivity takes the form of deliberate choice. That choice need not, however, be rational. There are cases of "minimal choice," defined as *reward-sensitive choice*, that are not instances of rational choice.

To clarify this statement, I will try to provide explicit definitions of reward-sensitive choice and of rational choice. Consider first the idea of reward-sensitive choice. Suppose as above that the agent is faced with two feasible options, a and b, and does a. Imagine, moreover, a series of thought experiments in which the agent is faced with options a and b_1, a and b_2, a and b_3, ..., where b_i is b augmented with i dollars. If there exists an n such that for all $i < n$ the agent does a rather than b_i, whereas for all $i > n$ the agent does b_i rather than a, the initial action was due to a reward-sensitive choice; if there is no such n, it was not. This test presupposes, controversially, that there is a trade-off between money and all other goods. If the utility of money has an upper bound or if some other good is viewed as lexicographically superior to money, this will not be the case. The test yields sufficient conditions, but they are not necessary. I believe that similar problems would arise for any attempt to define the idea of reward-sensitive choice in purely behavioral terms. Although we know intuitively what it means to choose on the basis of expected rewards, there are so many different kinds of rewards that can motivate an agent that no single test will work for all of them. Once we know what motivates an agent, we can design a test, but in that case we would not need it.

Rational Choice

The proposition that an action is based on *rational* choice is even more difficult to establish on the basis on direct behavioral criteria. As will be explained in a moment, for an action to be rational it has to stand in specific relations to the desires, beliefs, and information sets of the agent. To impute these mental states to him, we must rely on behavioral evidence, including verbal behavior. Yet to take the step from behavior to mental states, we must also assume that the agent is by and large rational.[5] Without that assumption, we would be at a total loss. When we know, for instance, that an agent is in possession of certain bits of information, we automatically infer that he holds the belief that they warrant, but only because we assume, in an equally automatic way, that he is rational. Assuming that he holds the belief, we can then proceed to assess a particular piece of behavior as rational or irrational. Alternatively, we may assume that the behavior was rational, impute to him the beliefs that would make it rational, and then assess those beliefs as rational or irrational in light of his information.[6] The choice between these two procedures depends (among other things) on their outcomes. If the first procedure makes his behavior appear grossly irrational and the second makes his beliefs appear mildly irrational, we prefer the latter.[7] Clearly, these are matters of interpretation that cannot be reduced to a mechanical test.

The basic model of rational choice is set out in figure 5.1. Here the arrows have both a causal interpretation and a normative one. A rational action, for instance, is one that is both caused by the desires and beliefs of the agents and optimal in the light of these desires and beliefs. The blocked arrow, about which more later, indicates a causal link that is proscribed on normative grounds.

The model involves three distinct levels of optimality. First, for an action to be rational, it has to be the best means of satisfying the desires of the agent, given his beliefs. In itself, this is a very weak requirement. If I want to kill a person and I believe that the best way of doing so is to make a doll representing him and stick a pin through it, then according to this weak definition I act rationally if I make the doll and pierce it with a pin. We would hardly be satisfied with this conclusion, however, not because my homicidal desire is irrational (it may be immoral, but that is another matter), but because my belief is transparently ill-founded.

Second, therefore, we need to stipulate that the beliefs themselves are rational, in the sense of being grounded in the information available to the agent. These may be beliefs about factual matters or about gen-

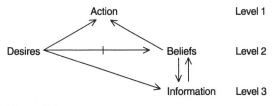

Figure 5.1
Basic model of rational choice.

eral lawlike connections. In particular, they will include beliefs about the *opportunities* available to the agent. In fact, rational-choice theory is often stated in terms of desires and opportunities rather than desires and beliefs. In that "reduced" version, the theory says that a rational agent chooses the most-preferred element in his opportunity set. Sometimes this formulation is adequate enough. For some purposes, rational-choice theory can be summarized by saying that *people do as well as they can.* In general, however, we need to take account of the fact that the full set of objective opportunities available to the agent may not be known to him. Today, for instance, governments do not really know whether it is possible to develop commercially viable fusion power. Or, to take a more mundane example, a motorist arriving in an unknown city without a map will not know the full set of paths that will take him through it. Applied to this situation, the theory says that *people do as well as they believe they can.*

In such cases, the agent must use whatever information he has to form some belief or subjective estimate of the alternatives. The fact that it is subjective does not in itself detract from its rationality. On the contrary, *the concept of rationality is subjective through and through.*[8] To

be rational does not mean that one is invariably successful in realizing one's aims; it means only that one has
no reason, after the fact, to think that one should have
acted differently. Nor does a rational belief have to be
true; it must only be well grounded in the available
information. Beliefs are rational if they are formed by
procedures that (are believed to) produce more true
beliefs in the long run than any alternative procedure,
but on any particular occasion the belief thus formed
may not correspond to the facts. Beliefs are irrational
when they are shaped by distorting influences of various kinds. Some of these are more in the nature of mistakes, as when people fail to observe simple principles
of statistical inference. Others, however, belong to the
category of *motivated irrationality*, as when the adding-
up errors made by a salesman systematically (although
nonintentionally) work out to his favor.

However, a belief is not made rational simply by
being well grounded in the available information. If the
motorist is in a hurry, he should perhaps buy a map to
acquire more information about the feasible paths. At
the third level of optimality, therefore, the agent should
acquire an optimal amount of information, or more
accurately, invest an optimal amount of time, energy,
and money in gathering such information. Clearly, it
will often be irrational not to invest any time in collect-
ing information. If one is buying a house or a car, one
should compare several options and investigate each of
them in some depth. Equally clearly, there are occasions
when there is a danger of gathering too much information. If a doctor makes too many tests before deciding
on treatment, the patient may die under his hands. A
general who insists on accurate information about the

able to escape the belief trap. Although behavior based on these beliefs may look strange to an outside observer, it is perfectly rational.

The idea of a belief trap can be generalized to cover situations in which agents lack beliefs about the expected costs and benefits of gathering information relevant to their first-order beliefs *and* beliefs about the expected costs and benefits of gathering information relevant to their second-order beliefs, etc. A person arriving in a foreign country with mistaken preconceived notions about how it works might be prevented by these very notions from finding out how it really works.

Clearly, minimal choice need not be rational. In fact, minimal choice is consistent with irrationality at each of the three levels of optimization shown in figure 5.1. A person may be sensitive to the expected rewards from action even if the expectations are formed in an irrational manner or based on suboptimal investment in information. Moreover, reward sensitivity is consistent with failure to choose the best means to realize one's desires, given one's beliefs. Suppose that a person is tempted to embezzle money from his firm, although he believes that all things considered, it is more prudent to abstain. We may imagine that he sticks to his decision until, one day, he finds himself in a position to embezzle a very large amount. He continues to believe that all things considered, he should not do it, but the temptation is now so strong that it overrides his all-things-considered judgment. By construction, he is both reward-sensitive and akratic: he conforms to the canons of minimal choice, but not to those of rational choice.

enemy's movement before attacking can easily be taken by surprise. In between these extremes, there exists an optimal level of search, a "golden mean." Whether one can *know* where this optimum is located is another matter, which I shall not discuss here.[9]

At any given time, an individual will have certain beliefs about the costs and value of acquiring new information. What he does must be assessed in the light of those beliefs, not in the light of what an external observer might deem optimal. The eye cannot see farther than its horizon. We can, therefore, give a third and final statement of rational-choice theory: the principle that *people make the most out of what they have*, including their beliefs and their preferences. The radically subjective implications of this idea are discussed below.

As shown in figure 5.1, there are several factors that determine the amount of information that a rational agent will gather. The agent's beliefs about the expected costs and expected value of gathering the information will obviously matter. His desires, that is, how important the decision is to him, will also enter into the calculus. Indirectly, therefore, the desires of the agents will enter into the process of belief formation. The blocked arrow from desires to beliefs in figure 5.1 is intended to indicate that a direct influence, as in wishful thinking, is inadmissible. Although Hume said, "Reason is, and ought only to be the slave of the passions,"[10] he did not mean that passion should be allowed to set itself up as an arbitrary tyrant. Even a slave needs some independence to serve his master well; beliefs born of passion serve passion badly.[11]

Let me make two remarks to underline the subjective nature of rationality. To anticipate section 5.3 below, consider first drug addiction. One reason that addiction can be rational in Gary Becker's model of addiction is the low weight that addicts place on future gratifications compared to present ones. That weight—expressed in the rate of time discounting—is not itself subject to rational assessment. A time preference is just another preference. Some like chocolate ice cream, whereas others have a taste for vanilla: this is just a brute fact, and it would be absurd to say that one preference is more rational than the other. Similarly, it is just a brute fact that some like the present, whereas others have a taste for the future. If a person discounts the future very heavily, consuming an addictive substance may, for that person, be a form of rational behavior.

The argument may seem counterintuitive. I believe, however, that if we want to explain behavior on the bare assumption that people make the most out of what they have, the idea is exactly right. If some individuals have the bad luck to be born with genes, or be exposed to external influences, that make them discount the future heavily, behavior with long-term self-destructive consequences may, for them, be their best option. We cannot expect them to take steps to reduce their rate of time discounting, because to want to be motivated by long-term concerns ipso facto *is* to be motivated by long-term concerns.[12] To be sure, addicts have no *reason* to discount the future heavily. The date at which a good becomes available does not in itself constitute a reason for wanting or preferring it. If we disregard such facts as that we know that but not when we shall die and that we will enjoy things less when we grow old, any year is as good as any other. Yet the lack of reasons for discounting the future does not detract from the explanatory power of discounting.[13]

A different issue is whether *changes* in the rate of discounting may be viewed as irrational. If, under the influence of some visceral factor (pain, emotion, cravings, thirst), the agent pays reduced attention to the long-term consequences of present choice, this effect may come about in two ways. On the one hand, these consequences might simply not be present on his cognitive horizon; on the other, they might be present but devalued in comparison with short-term rewards. On virtually any account of rationality, the former phenomenon would be an instance of irrationality. It seems somewhat arbitrary, then, to refrain from using the same label for the latter. For some writers, in fact, discounting *means* that distant prospects lose some of the cognitive vividness by virtue of which they can motivate behavior in the present.[14] These are subtle matters, and our vocabulary for dealing with them is inadequate. I am inclined to say, nevertheless, that any viscerally induced and behaviorally manifested disregard for the future is a sign of irrationality, regardless of the exact mechanism by which the effect is produced.

Consider next belief formation. Gerry Mackie argues,

Women who practice infibulation [a form of female genital mutilation] are caught in a belief trap. The Bambara of Mali believe that the clitoris will kill a man if it comes in contact with the penis during intercourse. In Nigeria, some groups believe that if a baby's head touches the clitoris during delivery, the baby will die. I call these self-enforcing beliefs: a belief that cannot be revised, because *the believed costs of testing the belief are too high.*[15]

If a person has the bad luck of growing up in a society in which these second-order beliefs about the cost of testing first-order beliefs are widely held, he will not be

Summary

Bodily movements can be classified along a spectrum. At one extreme are the reflex behaviors that do not involve cognition at all. At the other extreme we find actions produced by deliberate rational choice that satisfies the three optimality conditions that I stated above. Whereas most will admit that there is at least one intermediate category, I have argued that there may be two distinct such categories. Closer to the first end of the spectrum we find behavior that is intentional but reward-insensitive. Although hard evidence for such behavior may be difficult to find, I do not believe the possibility can be excluded. Closer to the other end we find behavior that is reward-sensitive but not rational. This case is much less controversial. In the intermediate cases, visceral states such as pain, thirst, emotions, and addictive cravings can play an important role.

5.2   Choice and Emotion

The relation between choice and emotion is threefold. First, can we choose our emotions? Second, how do emotions affect the rationality of choice? Third, when emotion and interest pull us in different reactions, how do they interact to produce choice?

Choosing Emotions

As I said in section 3.3 above, I believe that the occurrence of emotions is basically unbidden. Not only do we not choose (minimally or rationally) to have emotions; emotions are not even actions. There are, to be sure, writers who have argued the opposite. Both Jean-Paul Sartre and Roy Schafer claim, from different premises and probably with different meanings in mind, that emotions are chosen.[16] Richard Solomon has even argued that emotions are *rationally* chosen. "Every emotion is a subjective strategy for the maximization of personal dignity and self-esteem."[17] For instance, anger promotes self-esteem because it is always tinged with self-righteousness, except when it is directed against oneself, as in guilt.[18] The latter emotion contributes to self-esteem because "the ability to admit and atone for our mistakes is . . . essential to wisdom and personal dignity." And so on, down a list of some thirty-odd emotions. Elsewhere I offer a range of arguments against these views,[19] and I shall not repeat them here. In my opinion, there is no doubt that common sense has got it right: emotions are involuntarily undergone rather than consciously chosen, events rather than actions.

That being said, there are a number of marginal and indirect senses in which emotions are under the control of the will. These techniques all presuppose that we are dealing with proper emotions rather than with proto-emotions section (4.2). This statement may not be rigorously true. When an emotion is misdiagnosed (as when depression is mistaken for fatigue) rather than unacknowledged (as when an angry person is unaware of being in any kind of special state), the agent might be motivated and able to affect it. Yet the practical importance of this qualification is limited. At least in the cases that I have come across, attempts to control an emotion presuppose awareness of the emotion as such.

First, rather than choosing directly to have (or not to have) certain emotions, one may choose situations in which they will predictably be produced (or predictably not be produced). One of Solomon's examples actually points in this direction. He offers the vignette of "a woman [who] continues to patronize a shop which she knows has cheated her [because] her small losses are more than compensated for by the self-righteous satisfaction of her continuing indignation."[20] Rather than supporting his theoretical argument, however, the story directly undermines it. It suggests that the woman chooses to get into a certain situation because it predictably—that is, *independently* of her will—generates the gratifying emotion of indignation.

The negative version of this strategy—avoiding certain situations to avoid the emotions they would produce—is common and effective. The positive version, however, has its limits. Unlike hedonic experiences, such as those provided by good food, or aesthetic experiences, such as those provided by a beautiful sunset, most emotional experiences are greatly magnified if they take us by surprise. But one cannot plan for surprise, any more than one can tickle oneself into laughing. As an illustration, consider sports-generated satisfaction. In 1994 Norway organized the Winter Olympics, where Norwegian participants won a large number of gold medals. In an ex post assessment of the value of this event for the Norwegian population, the sheer emotional exuberance generated by the Norwegian winners would be a major item on the income side of the balance sheet. It seems plausible that these emotional gains by themselves were large enough to justify the huge construction expenses. Yet because this experience could not have been planned, the expenses may not have been justified ex ante. The point is not that nobody could count on the Norwegians being so successful. It is that if their victories *had* been predictable, they would have generated much less excitement. If the actual emotional satisfaction from Norwegian success in the games was a decreasing function $f(p)$ of the ex ante probability p of Norwegian success, the expected emotional satisfaction $p \times f(p)$ may have been too small to justify the investment, for the actual p or even for any p.

Second, we can also create emotions without any external stimulus. Within limits, it is possible to stimulate emotions deliberately by remembering (or imagining) situations in which they arose (or would arise) spontaneously. Arlie Hochschild tells, for instance, how one air stewardess handles angry passengers by seeking to feel compassion rather than anger: "I pretend something traumatic has happened in their lives. Once I had an irate that was complaining about me, cursing at me, threatening to get my name and report me to the company. I later found out that his son had just died. Now when I meet an irate I think of that man."[21] Yet as Hochschild also observes, this technique is parasitic on genuine emotion: "To remember experiences emotively, he or she must first experience them in that way too."[22] By exploiting the feedback from emotional expressions to the emotions themselves, we can elicit an emotion by performing the verbal and nonverbal behaviors that normally express it.[23] As Montaigne noted, professional orators and professional mourners may end up experiencing the emotions they are paid to express.[24] Yet these cases too are parasitic on normal or spontaneous occurrences.

Third, one may be able to control the emotion. Often, it is possible to block an emotion at the outset. Even when a pang of envy at the sight of another's greater possession or success arises spontaneously in the mind, we may nip it in the bud by thinking about something else or mentally shrugging our shoulders. Also, we may choose to suppress the physiological expression of the emotion, to prevent an amplifying feedback to the emotion itself. Although the emotion arises independently in the mind, its further course can be subject to choice. Yet in an important class of cases, conscious control may not be feasible if awareness of the emotion comes later than the "point of no return" (section 2.3). As we shall see, when an emotion is not under the control of choice, it may also be an obstacle to (minimal or rational) choice.

Fourth, even if one cannot choose to have (or not to have) an occurrent emotion, one could try to develop (or curb) a disposition for that emotion to occur. This strategy has been recommended by a number of writers, ranging from Stoic and Buddhist philosophers to modern psychotherapists. In the past, its main purpose was to curb dispositions to be afraid, angry, and the like. In its modern versions, there is also the positive purpose of developing emotional dispositions whose absence is deplored. Some people complain of being unable to love or to grieve and seek professional help to overcome their problem.

For strategies of character planning to be rational ex ante, three conditions must be fulfilled. First, there must exist an efficient and reliable technology of emotional planning. Second, the course of external events should be reasonably predictable. Occurrent emotions are jointly caused by emotional dispositions and events that are outside the agent's control, and if the latter can-

not be foreseen, there may not be much point in modifying the former. A stoic attitude may be useful if one
goes bankrupt but might otherwise be a killjoy. And
third, the cost of using the technology should not
exceed the benefits. In the case of psychotherapy, there
is no need to discuss the satisfaction of the second and
third conditions, as the first is manifestly not satisfied.
An important study by Robyn Dawes shows that with
the exception of some forms of behavioral therapy, psychotherapy essentially does not offer any benefits over
and above those that would be provided by talking with
any warm and interested person.[25]

The Impact of Emotion on Choice

Following the analyses in sections 2.4 and 5.1, we may
ask whether and when emotion (1) induces behavior
that is instinctual rather than intentional, (2) leaves
intentionality intact but undermines reward sensitivity
(action without choice), (3) leaves reward sensitivity
intact but undermines rationality (minimal but not
rational choice), or (4) leaves rationality intact. Going
beyond those analyses, we may ask (5) whether emotions could actually enhance rationality.

I first ask, then, whether emotionally shaped behavior is always voluntary or intentional, that is, consti-
tutes *action* rather than instinctual or reflex behavior.
The findings of LeDoux cited in section 2.4 above show
that this is not invariably the case. Some emotions are
(a) triggered by perception rather than cognition and
(b) trigger behavior by "automatic pilot" rather than
by "willful control."[26] Although it remains to be seen
whether these two features are found in other emotions

besides fear, it is plausible that anger, distress, and sexual arousal (if that counts as an emotion) generate behavior in similar nonintentional ways. It seems reasonable to assume that (b) will not obtain in the absence of (a). If the thinking part of the brain is part of the mechanism that triggers the emotion, it would seem plausible that it is also involved in the mechanism by which the emotion triggers behavior. But this is guesswork, and I might be wrong.

Next I ask whether emotion can induce intentional action that is reward-insensitive. Once again, fear provides an example. A person running away from an approaching lion may be so consumed with fear that he does not notice or call to mind that he is heading toward a cliff, which represents an even greater certainty of death. In terminology that differs from mine but is easily translated into it, Nico Frijda suggests vividly how *fear* may generate what I have called "action without choice," that is, behavior that is intentional but not guided by consequences:

Action tendencies [of emotions] can be said to differ from intentions . . . in that the desired, to-be-achieved, to-be-maintained, or to-be-regained situation is not a true goal. It is not an anticipated future state to be achieved, but one that should obtain *now*. . . . Action tendency generated by an event that blocks freedom of action aims at removing the obstacle rather than regaining freedom. Panicky flight is directed, not toward a place of safety, but away from the place of danger. Desire pushes away from the state of not-yet-possessing, rather than toward that of possessing; it aims at crossing the distance to the object, rather than being guided by the prospect of the achieved embrace, at least in a naive subject. Intention, by contrast, does strive toward regained freedom, a place of safety, or the prospect of possessing. Action tendencies are pushed by the feelings of pain, current pleasure or desire, and the control precedence they impose; intentions are pulled by goal anticipations without such imposed control precedence.[27]

Anger offers similar examples. The dynamic illustrated below in figure 5.2 may prevent the agent from controlling his emotion, and once he is in full flight of anger, he may not be able to control his behavior, even in the face of likely adverse consequences. In war, for instance, anger can enable soldiers to face certain or highly likely death. Montaigne comments, "Aristotle says that choler sometimes serves virtue and valour as a weapon. That is most likely; nevertheless those who deny it have an amusing reply: it must be some new-fangled weapon; for we wield the other weapons: that one wields us; it is not our hand that guides it: it guides our hand; it gets a hold on us: not we on it."[28] Below, I suggest that *shame* has the capacity for blotting out concerns with future outcomes. *Sexual arousal* too may induce behavior oblivious to all other concerns, short perhaps of the interest in short-term physical survival. Unlike fear, anger, and shame, it is unlikely to be *fully* reward-insensitive.

Third, we may inquire into the capacity of emotions to undermine rationality while leaving reward sensitivity intact. In my discussion of the interaction between emotion and interest below, I sketch a semiformal account of this phenomenon in terms of catastrophe theory. No formalism is needed, however, to see that it is quite common. As Frijda notes, emotions affect "probability and credibility estimates" concerning events outside one's control and also "cause some measure of belief in the efficacy of actions one would not believe in under other conditions."[29] Although Frijda does not mention that emotions may also subvert the process of information acquisition, the fact that passion can make us jump to conclusions is too obvious to need stressing. What should be stressed, however, is that this occurs not only in the face of threatening events, when the expected opportunity costs of gathering information are so high that delays would be irrational. *Any* strong emotion creates a tendency to act immediately, even if nothing would be lost and something might be gained by pausing to find out more about the situation. The urge of a guilty person to seek relief by making atonement may be so strong that he does not take the time to find out what form of atonement might be in the victim's best interest. A person in love may marry in haste, being too impatient to find out whether the love object might have some unknown and perhaps less than wonderful qualities.

Yet even a man whose love for a woman wrongly leads him to interpret her behavior as a sign that the feeling is requited or to believe that he can make her love him by parading before her window may hesitate to act on his feelings if he has a rival who is known to have beaten up other suitors. He may be irrational, but he is also reward-sensitive. The emotion distorts his cognition, but not the point of blotting out all consideration of consequences. In an alternative perspective, one might argue that emotion raises the rate of time discounting, but not to the point where future consequences of present action are totally ignored.

Fourth, emotion may leave the capacity for rational decision making entirely intact. This is trivially true for very mild emotions, but it can be true for strong emotions too. Aristotle argued that *hatred*, for instance, as distinct from *anger*, was consistent with rationality. "The angry are more impetuous in making an attack, for they do not follow rational principle. And men are very apt to give way to their passions when they are insulted. ... Hatred is more reasonable, for anger is accompanied by pain, which is an impediment to reason, whereas hatred is painless."[30] Although the last claim is implausible, the contrast is broadly valid. The greatest act of hatred in history was the Holocaust, which was carried out in a very efficient and rational manner. Some forms of anger too are compatible with deliberate, calculating behavior, as reflected in the saying that revenge is a dish that is best when eaten cold. A person who is passionately in love may remain perfectly lucid about his prospects and in full control of his behavior, as illustrated by (most aspects of) Julien Sorel's behavior toward Mathilde de la Mole in *Le Rouge et le noir*. There is no universal law of human nature expressing an inverse relation between passion and reason, though there may well be a negative statistical correlation.

Throughout the 25 centuries in which these issues have been discussed, it has in fact been assumed that emotion tends to detract from rational thought and rational choice. Until very recently, nobody, to my knowledge, has argued that emotion could actually *improve* the rationality of thinking and of decisions. In the last few decades, however, several arguments to that effect have been put forward. The commonly cited idea of a bell-shaped relation between arousal—including emotional arousal—and task performance seems to have limited support.[31] Findings about a positive relation between pleasurable emotions and performance may be more robust,[32] although perhaps limited by the somewhat trivial nature of many experiments (good emotions are induced by giving subjects a pack of candy).

A number of recent writers have also argued that emotions are indispensable for rational decision making, since they enable individuals to make up their mind in situations that are too complex to be handled by rational analysis of options and their consequences.[33] For one thing, emotions enable us to avoid procrastination—to make *some* decision when that is what matters rather than making the optimal decision. For another, in some cases the emotions can actually help us make the *best* decision. I have stated my arguments against these views elsewhere,[34] and I shall only summarize them briefly here. The idea that emotions or "gut feelings" are superior to rational choice rests on a caricature of the latter idea. Also, the evidence adduced for a *causal link* between emotions and good decision making in fact only supports the claim of a *correlation* between flat emotions and bad decision making in patients with brain lesions, which thus leaves open the possibility that both might be caused by the organic damage. Overall, therefore, I conclude that the thesis of emotions as enhancers of rationality remains unproven. It may turn out to be true, but more evidence is needed.

Emotion and Interest

An issue that partially overlaps the preceding one concerns how emotions interact with other motivations to generate behavior. Among the latter, I shall consider only material self-interest ("interest" for short), although similar problems arise for the relation between emotions and impartial motivations. For instance, a wealthy liberal might prefer on impartial grounds to send his children to a public school, but his emotional attachment to the children might induce a preference for a better-quality private education.

Among economists, the most common way of modeling the interaction between emotions and interests is to view the former as psychic costs or benefits that enter into the utility function on a par with satisfactions derived from material rewards.[35] To explore this idea, assume that a person is tempted to steal a book from the library. If he feels guilty about doing it, he may abstain. If he steals the book and then feels guilt, he may return the book to the library. If guilt is modeled as a cost, both abstention from stealing and return of the book would be explained by a simple cost-benefit analysis. This approach has the great advantage that it allows us to account for the undeniable existence of a trade-off between moral emotions and self-interest. The world is not made up of two exclusive and exhaustive categories: those who would steal a book whenever there was no risk of detection and those who would never do so. Many people would go ahead and steal the book if but only if its value to them was sufficiently high and/or its value to others sufficiently small. To model such behavior, we could talk as if guilt and interest add up to an inclusive utility, with the marginal disutility from guilt being an increasing function of (say) the number of people on the waiting list for the book and the marginal utility from interest being a decreasing function of (say) the time the agent expects to use the book.

Whether or not this model of the interaction between emotion and interest is predictively adequate, I submit that it is basically flawed. If guilt were nothing but an anticipated or experienced cost, an agent whose guilt deters him from stealing or retaining the book should be willing to buy a guilt-erasing pill if it were sufficiently cheap. *I submit that no person capable of being deterred by guilt would buy the pill.* In fact, he would feel guilty about buying it. For him, taking the pill in order to escape guilt and be able to steal the book would be as morally bad as just stealing it. He would not see any moral relevance between stealing the book in a two-step operation (taking the pill to steal the book) and stealing it in a one-step operation. There is a strict analogy between this argument and a point that I have made elsewhere, namely that a person who discounts the future very highly would not be motivated to buy a pill that would reduce his rate of time discounting.[36] To want to be motivated by remote consequences of present behavior *is* to be motivated by remote consequences of present behavior. Similarly, to want to be immoral *is* to be immoral. A person willing to take the guilt-erasing pill does not need it.

We thus need a model that can account for the trade-off between guilt and interest and yet does not imply that a reluctant agent would buy the guilt-erasing pill. I conjecture that the model would involve some kind of nonintentional psychic causality rather than deliberate choice. To illustrate what I have in mind, I shall sketch a model drawn from catastrophe theory along the lines of a model of the relation between personal opinion and conformism proposed by Abraham Tesser and John Achee.[37] In a catastrophe model, the surface describing

the behavior of a dependent variable as a function of
two independent variables folds in on itself in a cusp.
Within a certain range, a given constellation of the independent variables is thus consistent with several values
of the dependent variable.

Suppose that the agent is initially unwilling to steal
the book but that as its value to him increases, he finally
decides to do so.[38] Suppose conversely that the agent
has stolen the book, but that as its value to others
increases, he finally returns it to the library. In the first
case, suppose that its value to others is 10 and that he
decides to steal it just when its value to him reaches 15.
In the second case, suppose that its initial value to him
is 15 and the initial value to others is 6. On the cost-
benefit model, he would return it when its value to others reaches 10. On the catastrophe model, he might not
do so until its value to others reached 15. The reason
for this asymmetry is found in the mechanism of dissonance reduction.[39] An individual who is subject to several motivations that point in different directions will
feel an unpleasant feeling of tension. When, on balance,
he favors one action, he will try to reduce the tension by
looking for cognitions that support it; when he favors
another, he will look for cognitions that stack the balance of arguments in favor of that action.[40] Thus the
timing of the switch in behavior will be path-depen-
dent.

Dissonance theory is more realistic than the cost-benefit model in that it views individuals as making hard
choices on the basis of *reasons* rather than on the basis
of introspections about how they feel. The person who
has stolen the book but feels guilty about it may try to
alleviate his guilt by coming up with additional reasons

that justify his behavior rather than by accepting a guilt-erasing pill. It is a fundamental feature of human beings that they have an image of themselves as *acting for a reason*. Guilt, in this perspective, acts not as a cost but as a psychic force that induces the individual to rationalize his behavior. Beyond a certain point, when the arguments on the other side become too strong and the rationalization breaks down, a switch in behavior occurs. Although we may well say that the switch occurs when the guilt becomes unbearable, we should add that the point at which it becomes unbearable is itself influenced, and in fact delayed, by the guilt. This *dual role of emotions in decision making* is an important phenomenon.

As indicated, the "tension" in this example would be guilt if the person on balance preferred to steal the book, and perhaps regret if he preferred to abstain from stealing it. As psychologists have not considered emotions as sources of cognitive dissonance and of dissonance reduction, the argument involves an extension of dissonance theory as usually stated. Yet there seems to be no reason why emotions could not be sources of dissonance. Although it is descriptively accurate that dissonance theory places the "emphasis on the individual's concept of *what he is* rather than his concept of *what he should be*,"[41] this limitation on the scope of the theory seems arbitrary.

An analysis of shame suggests another alternative to the simple cost-benefit model. Empirically, we know that people can take extreme actions when targeted for social ostracism. The recent case of the American Navy Admiral who killed himself when it was shown that he was not entitled to decorations he was wearing is one example.[42] The six Frenchmen who killed themselves in 1997 after they had been caught in a crackdown on pedophilia is another. The question is whether the shame entered into their decision merely as a cost or in some other way.

On the cost-benefit model, the suicide would be explained by stipulating that the present pain from shame is greater than the discounted present value of the next-best option, such as moving to another location and assuming a new name. It is hard to refute this account, as the disutility of shame can always be stipulated to be arbitrarily high. Yet observation and introspection suggest that this is not all there is to the story. Intense feelings of shame tend to blot out, or at least seriously impair, any consideration of the future. In extreme cases, the person suffering from intense shame may not think beyond the present moment at all. All he wants is immediate release. This would be a case of reward insensitivity. In less extreme cases, the person is able to think about the future but attaches less importance to it than he would under normal circumstances, either because he cannot fully imagine that the shame will fade away[43] or because he suffers a temporary heightening of his rate of time discounting. The shame enters both as a cost in the present and as a causal force affecting the assessment of future benefits. This is another instance of the dual role of emotion in decision making.

Summary

Although emotions themselves cannot be chosen, one can affect them indirectly by seeking out or avoiding the conditions under which they occur, by giving in to or resisting their characteristic expressions, and by cultivating dispositions to have them. A yet more central connection lies in the impact of emotion on choice. The emotions have two features—arousal and valence—by virtue of which they can affect the conditions for choice in general and for rational choice in particular. The feeling of urgency bestowed by many emotions—even when there is no need to act swiftly— can interfere with rational acquisition of information. In extreme cases, the action tendency associated with the emotion may blot out considerations of other options and of long-term consequences. Emotions can also sustain wishful thinking and, more mysteriously, counterwishful thinking of the kind displayed by Othello. When emotions coexist with other motivations, they often play a dual role in generating behavior. The role of emotions cannot be reduced to that of shaping the reward parameters for rational choice; they also affect the ability to make rational choices within those parameters. This *dual role of the emotions*—shaping choices as well as rewards—has analogues in pain, addictive cravings, and other visceral factors. As in these other cases, the claim is not that the emotions fully determine choice or that there is no trade-off between emotional rewards and other rewards. Rather, it is that the trade-off itself is modified by one of the rewards that are traded off against the others.

5.3   Choice and Addiction

The relation between addiction and choice has several aspects. First, we may ask whether addiction affects the capacity for making choices or, more specifically, for making rational choices. Next, we may ask whether addiction could result from choice or, more specifically, from rational choice. Third, we may ask about the role of choice in overcoming addiction.

The impact of addiction on minimal choice

It is often claimed that addicts have an overwhelming, overpowering, or irresistible urge to consume, in other words, that they are reward-insensitive. Benjamin Rush offered a dramatic illustration: "When strongly urged, by one of his friends, to leave off drinking [a habitual drunkard] said, 'Were a keg of rum in one corner of a room, and were a cannon constantly discharging balls between me and it, I could not refrain from passing before that cannon, in order to get at the rum'."[44] Needless to say, nobody has actually carried out an experiment to see whether an alcoholic would literally risk his life to get to the next drink. As noted in section 4.3 above, the belief in the irresistibility of drugs may be a convenient excuse rather than an accurate causal diagnosis. Although one cannot exclude that some alcoholics may on occasion experience such craving that they are literally oblivious to everything else, the literature on alcoholism does not suggest this to be a common event. In "one of the more realistic studies, alcoholics were given free 'priming' drinks and then offered incentives for not drinking further. Larger priming drinks were more likely to lead to a binge. However, for every priming dose there was an incentive that would promote self-control."[45]

A more plausible case may be made for the reward

insensitivity of cocaine addicts. Frank Gawin writes, "Cocaine addicts report that virtually all thoughts are focused on cocaine during binges; nourishment, sleep, money, loved ones, responsibility and survival lose all significance."[46] In a vivid example offered by Eliot Gardner and James David, Jeannette, an inner-city woman, has been invited to a crack party:

Jeannette goes to the party and begins to smoke the crack. At first she attempts to pace her drug use, using more beer than crack. But the *intense* pleasure of each crack "hit" inhalation overwhelms her. Within a short time her cocaine use increases dramatically, and takes on an insistent and frantic quality; she grabs for the crack pipe out of turn, and pleads for extra "hits" of the crack cocaine smoke. . . . She is *totally* focused on obtaining the desired drug. Her money and trade goods exhausted, she begins to perform sex acts for money. By the time the crack is exhausted and the party over, she has performed multiple sex acts on total strangers, in full view of other participants, for as little as a single "hit" of crack.[47]

The clinical picture of cocaine addiction involves, among other things, lack of interest in food and often heavy weight loss. In this sense, cocaine does, as Gawin says, take precedence over survival. Yet the lack of interest in eating only shows indifference to long-term negative consequences of present behavior. It does not show that the agent is insensitive to *other short-term costs*, such as the risk of death from cannon balls being discharged across the room. The idea of total reward insensitivity is an extremely demanding one. As noted in section 5.1 above, it may be hard (and ethically indefensible) to carry out the experiments that would allow us to determine whether there exists a cost c, to be incurred with probability p within time interval t, that would deter the agent from giving in to the putative irresistible desire. To any negative finding one may always counter that reward sensitivity could be demonstrated for higher c, higher p, or lower t.

In economic analysis, the issue of reward sensitivity is often stated as a question of *price elasticity*. The demand for a good is said to be totally inelastic if the same amount is bought regardless of price (on the assumption that the total cost is within the consumer's budget). If a price increase causes less of the good to be bought (under the same assumption), the demand is said to be elastic. Thus a diabetic's demand for insulin might be totally inelastic, whereas normal consumer demand for chocolate is highly elastic. The question is whether addictive drugs are more like insulin or more like chocolate. Although this question is hard to answer in the case of illegal drugs, the data on legal drugs show considerable price elasticity. In the case of alcohol, which is mainly consumed by nonaddicts, this finding might be compatible with the demand of heavy drinkers and alcoholics being inelastic. This interpretation is refuted, however, by the fact that the incidence of cirrhosis of the liver (a good indicator of alcoholism) falls when liquor taxes go up.[48] In the case of nicotine, which is mainly consumed by addicts, the data are more unambiguous. By and large, for every one percent increase in the price of cigarettes, consumption falls by one half percent.[49]

The elasticity findings do not speak directly to the issue of "irresistible" desires. For one thing, the budget assumption may not always be fulfilled. "Due to the food shortage during the First World War, the price of Danish aquavit was raised more than 10 times over, while the price of beer was doubled. These drastic measures reduced per capita consumption of alcohol by three quarters, from 6.7 to 1.6 litres, within 2 years."[50] This effect may have been due in part to the inability of heavy drinkers to finance their habit. For another, we may want to distinguish within-episode from between-episode behavior. An alcoholic or a crack addict in the middle of a binge may be less reward-sensitive than the same person when he is recovering from the binge and thinking about his future. The between-episode behavior of "Jeannette" was much more controlled than her within-episode behavior (described above). This is not to say that between-episode cravings are not intense, whether they are triggered by memory of the drug euphoria or by sudden exposure to cues associated with drug taking, only that they are more reward-sensitive than those that arise under the direct influence of the drug.

The Impact of Addiction On Rational Choice

Concerning the impact of addiction on minimal choice, my conclusion is agnostic. Whereas I do believe that emotions have the capacity for short-circuiting all concern for consequences and alternatives, I am not sure that addictive cravings do. What seems abundantly clear, however, is that these cravings can undermine the agent's capacity for making *rational* choices. Drug-induced irrationality can arise at all three levels in figure 5.1. In this diagram, desires serve as the unmoved mover, which is not itself subject to rationality assessments. More controversially, one could also argue that addiction may induce irrationality by affecting the desires themselves.

Addiction has often been viewed as the paradigm of weakness of will, acting against one's own better judgment *at the time of acting*. As Donald Davidson has argued, a person can have a choice between x and y, have reasons for doing either, believe that the reasons for doing x are stronger, and yet do y.[51] A person who wants to quit drinking may nevertheless find himself accepting a drink when offered one at a party, knowing *as he does so* that he is acting against his own better judgment. The phrases I have italicized point to the need to distinguish drug-induced weakness of will from several other phenomena.

First, there is preference reversal due to hyperbolic discounting of the future. This mechanism is illustrated in figure 5.2. At time 1 the agent has a choice between a small reward that will be made available at time 2 and a larger reward that will be made available at time 3. The curves show how these future rewards are (hyperbolically) discounted to present value at earlier times. Before t^*, when the present-value curve of the larger reward (curve II) is above that of the smaller reward (curve I), the agent intends to choose the larger reward. After t^*, however, the present value of the smaller reward dominates. At time 2, he therefore chooses the smaller reward. According to George Ainslie, much of the ambivalence typically observed in addiction is due to this mechanism.[52] With the exponential discounting that is assumed in most economic models, such preference reversal can never occur: if an option is preferred at one time, it is preferred at all other times.

Whether hyperbolic discounting and the consequent preference reversal are instances of irrationality remains debatable. On the one hand, consistency is often enemy's movement before attacking can easily be taken by surprise. In between these extremes, there exists an optimal level of search, a "golden mean." Whether one can *know* where this optimum is located is another matter, which I shall not discuss here.[9]

At any given time, an individual will have certain beliefs about the costs and value of acquiring new information. What he does must be assessed in the light of those beliefs, not in the light of what an external observer might deem optimal. The eye cannot see farther than its horizon. We can, therefore, give a third and final statement of rational-choice theory: the principle that *people make the most out of what they have*, including their beliefs and their preferences. The radically subjective implications of this idea are discussed below.

As shown in figure 5.1, there are several factors that determine the amount of information that a rational agent will gather. The agent's beliefs about the expected costs and expected value of gathering the information will obviously matter. His desires, that is, how important the decision is to him, will also enter into the calculus. Indirectly, therefore, the desires of the agents will enter into the process of belief formation. The blocked arrow from desires to beliefs in figure 5.1 is intended to indicate that a direct influence, as in wishful thinking, is inadmissible. Although Hume said, "Reason is, and ought only to be the slave of the passions,"[10] he did not mean that passion should be allowed to set itself up as an arbitrary tyrant. Even a slave needs some independence to serve his master well; beliefs born of passion serve passion badly.[11]

Let me make two remarks to underline the subjective nature of rationality. To anticipate section 5.3 below, consider first drug addiction. One reason that addiction can be rational in Gary Becker's model of addiction is the low weight that addicts place on future gratifications compared to present ones. That weight—expressed in the rate of time discounting—is not itself subject to rational assessment. A time preference is just another preference. Some like chocolate ice cream, whereas others have a taste for vanilla: this is just a brute fact, and it would be absurd to say that one preference is more rational than the other. Similarly, it is just a brute fact that some like the present, whereas others have a taste for the future. If a person discounts the future very heavily, consuming an addictive substance may, for that person, be a form of rational behavior.

The argument may seem counterintuitive. I believe, however, that if we want to explain behavior on the bare assumption that people make the most out of what they have, the idea is exactly right. If some individuals have the bad luck to be born with genes, or be exposed to external influences, that make them discount the future heavily, behavior with long-term self-destructive consequences may, for them, be their best option. We cannot expect them to take steps to reduce their rate of time discounting, because to want to be motivated by long-term concerns ipso facto *is* to be motivated by long-term concerns.[12] To be sure, addicts have no *reason* to discount the future heavily. The date at which a good becomes available does not in itself constitute a reason for wanting or preferring it. If we disregard such facts as that we know that but not when we shall die and that we will enjoy things less when we grow old, any year is as good as any other. Yet the lack of reasons for discounting the future does not detract from the explanatory power of discounting.[13]

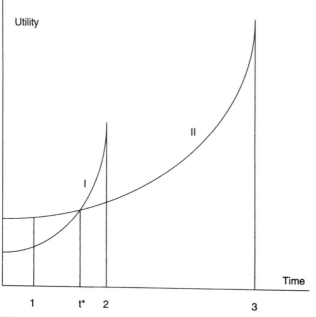

Figure 5.2

Preference reversal due to hyperbolic discounting of the future.

seen as a hallmark of rationality. On the other hand, if hyperbolic discounting is a hardwired feature of the organism, the principle " 'Ought' implies 'can' " suggests that it would be pointless to characterize it as irrational. The same comment applies to another source of preference reversal: cue dependence. A person may be firmly resolved to quit drinking until the sight and smell of a glass of whiskey induces a strong craving that enhances the value of a drink, quite independently of discounting. Given that craving, taking the drink may be quite rational; nor can the craving itself, being "unbidden," be said to be irrational.

In either variety, preference *reversal* is conceptually distinct from weakness of will, defined along Davidsonian lines as acting *against* your (all-things-considered) preference. A problem with Davidson's view is the difficulty of finding reliable evidence that the agent really thought that, all things considered, he should not take the drink. It is easy enough to find independent evidence that the person, *before* going to the party, wanted to abstain from drinking. He may have told his wife, for instance, "Stop me if I ask for a drink." *After* the party too, he may regret his behavior as contrary to his real interest and take steps to ensure that it doesn't happen again. But how can we know that he holds this all-things-considered judgment at the very moment that he is accepting the drink? By assumption, there is no observable behavior that can support this interpretation. How can we exclude the possibility of a preference reversal due to hyperbolic discounting? The agent might retain an accurate appreciation of the consequences of his behavior yet weigh them differently from how he did before.

The Davidsonian idea of weakness of will must also be distinguished from the case in which the agent does *not* retain an accurate appreciation of the consequences of his behavior. This corresponds to Aristotle's conception of weakness of will (or one of his conceptions), which admits "the possibility of having knowledge in a sense and yet not having it, as in the instance of a man asleep, mad, or drunk. But now this is just the condition of men under the influence of passions; for outbursts of anger and sexual appetites and some other such passions, it is evident, actually alter our bodily condition, and in some men even produce fits of madness. It is plain, then, that incontinent people must be said to be in a similar condition to these."[53] In a variant on this idea, we might assume that beliefs are *distorted* through drug-induced wishful thinking, rather than (as Aristotle seems to think) merely *clouded* by drug-induced arousal. Unlike the latter case, the former would be a case of what David Pears calls *motivated belief-formation*.[54] The resolution of the alcoholic to quit may break down if he is motivated to come up with a belief that justifies his drinking.

In the last few paragraphs I have sketched five ways of conceptualizing the ambivalence characteristic of many addicts:

- As preference reversal due to hyperbolic discounting
- As preference reversal due to cue-dependent cravings
- As Davidsonian weakness of will
- As Aristotelian weakness of will
- As Pearsian weakness of will

Although some of these mechanisms may not involve irrationality in a direct way, they all have an indirect link. An addict who wants to quit and then fails, for one of these reasons, may do so simply because he does not understand the causal forces that derail his resolution. After the fifth or the fiftieth attempt to quit, this lack of understanding itself becomes irrational. What began as simple ignorance turns into denials, excuses, and rationalizations. *The failure to learn from past failures* may be motivated by the desire to continue as an addict.

I now consider this issue—irrational belief formation in addicts—more generally, mainly with references to smoking and gambling. For addictive behavior to be rational, it must be based on rational beliefs about the consequences of engaging in it. If the beliefs are irrational, the distortion may or may not be due to the addictive behavior. On the one hand, some people may self-select into an addictive career because they have irrationally low estimates of the risks of smoking or, in the case of gambling, irrationally high estimates about the gains to be made. In these cases, there is no particular reason to expect the irrationality to be a motivated one. The biased estimates could well be due to one of the many "cold" mistakes in belief formation identified by Amos Tversky, Daniel Kahneman, and others.[55] On the other hand, the irrational belief might be induced by the desire to persist in the addictive behavior. Knowing the risks of smoking or gambling, a person might intend to engage in these activities at a moderate level, yet when he becomes hooked, his craving may induce a downward reassessment of the dangers involved (denial). To decide between these two hypotheses, one would have to observe the beliefs of smokers and gamblers before and after they became addicted. To my knowledge, there are no studies of this kind.

In the case of smoking, Kip Viscusi presents data on risk perception and finds that all categories of individuals have exaggerated beliefs about the risk of getting lung cancer from smoking but that the beliefs held by people who themselves smoke are closer to the correct values. He notes that if smokers have lower estimates, the cause may be either "the self-selection of people with low risk assessments into smoking" or "cognitive dissonance."[56] The former explanation fits well into a rational-choice model of addiction: people who smoke do so because they have, on average, a better understanding of the risks of smoking. The latter explanation relies on the motivated mechanism of dissonance reduction: because I smoke, smoking can't be so dangerous.[57] On this hypothesis, there would be two biases working in opposite directions. Smokers as well as nonsmokers are subject to misleading information about the dangers of smoking that induce exaggerated perceptions. At the same time, smokers are subject to a self-serving bias that induces them to discount the risks. Although the latter bias does not fully cancel the former, it does make the beliefs of smokers more nearly accurate than those of nonsmokers. It does not, however, make the beliefs more *rational*. From the point of view of rationality, being subject to two opposite biases is *worse* than being subject to only one of them.

Viscusi deals only with the perception that individuals have of the average risk of smoking, not with the perceived risk *to them*. In a study that addresses the latter question, F. P. McKenna finds evidence of self-serving bias in risk assessments by smokers and nonsmokers.[58] Individual smokers believe they are less likely than the average smoker to suffer health problems associated with smoking, such as lung cancer or heart disease. Individual nonsmokers have a similar belief with respect to average nonsmokers, although in their case the self-serving discrepancy is smaller. Whether these biases shape the beliefs that determine the initial decision to smoke or affect the beliefs once the decision has been made, they are clearly at odds with the idea of a rational smoker.[59]

In the case of gambling, consider first games of pure chance. Nongamblers and occasional gamblers can hardly fail to know that the expected monetary gains from casino gambling are negative. Most people are capable of grasping the commonsense idea that casinos could not make money, and hence would not exist, if gamblers consistently won. For the occasional gambler, the expected monetary loss is the price he pays for the thrill of gambling. Compulsive gamblers, however, seem to believe that they can beat the odds. Once again, we cannot tell for sure whether the irrational beliefs are the cause or the effect of the desire to gamble. Gamblers may be naturally superstitious or may become so to rationalize their behavior. Whatever the source of their irrationality, there is no question that gamblers are excessively optimistic. In fact, the "gambler's fallacy" is the very paradigm of erroneous statistical reasoning. This fallacy and its converse can be explained in terms of two heuristics of decision making:

When in a game there is a 50% chance of winning, people expect that a small number of rounds will also reflect this even chance. This is only possible when runs of gains and losses are short: a run of six losses would upset the local representativeness. This mechanism may explain the well-known gamblers fallacy: the expectation that the probability of winning increases with the length of an ongoing run of losses. The *representativeness heuristic* predicts that players will increase their bet after a run of losses, and decrease it after a run of gains. This is indeed what about half the players at blackjack tables do. . . . But the other half show the reverse behaviour: they increase their bets after winning, and decrease them after losing, which is predicted by the *availability heuristic*. After a run of losses, losing becomes the better available outcome, which may cause an overestimation of the probability of losing.[60]

Another important mechanism is the "psychology of the near win." When the outcome of the gamble is in some sense "close" to that on which the gambler had put his money, this is perceived as a confirmation of his beliefs. W. A. Wagenaar offers a graphic example:

[An] example of confirmation bias is the roulette player who suddenly places a large single bet on number 24, completely out of his routine betting pattern. His reason was that 12 is always followed by a 24. After he lost his bet I enquired what had gone wrong. He said: "It almost worked." The number that did come out was 15, which is adjacent to 24 on the number wheel. Probably he would have considered other outcomes like 5, 10, and 33 also confirmations, because they are nearby on the wheel. Also he could have taken the outcomes 22, 23, 25 and 26 as confirmations because their numerical value is close. Or the numbers 20, 21, 26 and 27, because they are adjacent on the tableau. Thus 13 out of 37 possible outcomes could be taken as confirmations of a rule that has no predictive value whatsoever. We can add to this number all the occasions on which 24 or another confirmatory number occurred, not immediately, but in the second round.[61]

Consider next games with an element of skill, such as betting on horses or point spreads. Here too we find a difference between occasional gamblers and regular ones. Thus "60 per cent of high-frequency [off-course betters] rated their bet selection as more than 50 per cent skill. The majority of less frequent betters rated their selection as 'all luck' or less than 25 per cent skill."[62] In addition to the self-selection explanation and the induced-bias explanation for this difference, there is also the possibility that regular gamblers are actually more skillful. Yet with the exception of professional gamblers, for whom the basic rule is to stick to plans made ahead of time, horse-race bettors tend to lose control when they get caught up in the excitement at the track. There is evidence not only that "as frequency of betting increases so does the belief that one's selection involves more skill" but also that "the observed behaviour actually becomes less skillful, with escalating stakes, hurried bet-selection and last minute changes in selection."[63] Alcohol has a similar dual effect of enhancing confidence in one's skill, for example, driving skill, while reducing actual skillfulness.

If the confirmation bias can operate in gambles of pure chance, it is obviously even more likely to be observed in gambles that involve a mix of chance and skill. At the roulette table, the concept of a near win is pure superstition. In games with handicapping, the idea of a near win has some evidential value, although less than what many gamblers believe. At the race track, choosing for a winner a horse that comes in second is seen both by the gambler himself and by others as proof that he was on to something.[64] When betting on professional football games, the "tendency to accept wins at face value but to transform losses into 'near wins' can produce overly optimistic assessments of one's gambling skill and the chances of future success."[65]

Consider next the rationality of addicts with respect to the issue of information. Do drug addicts invest optimally in information about what the drug is doing to their body? Do gamblers invest optimally in information that might improve their bets? I am unaware of any systematic discussion of these issues. Casual observation suggests, however, that drug addicts invest too little and gamblers too much in information. Concerning the latter claim, the very existence of the Monte Carlo *Revue Scientifique*, which logs successive outcomes at roulette, is proof that gamblers are willing to spend money gathering worthless information.[66] In games of pure chance, *any* investment in information is by definition excessive. Concerning the former claim, regular medical appointments to check on the status of one's liver or lungs are certainly not part of the behavioral pattern of heavy drinkers or smokers. Since there is wide publicity given to the health dangers posed by drugs, the suboptimal level of investment in information cannot be explained by assuming that the addicts are unaware that consumption might be dangerous. It seems reasonable to assume—although it has not been demonstrated—that they do not want to have the information, because they are afraid it might be bad news.

Up to this point I have kept to what I believe to be the standard model of rational choice, that shown in figure 5.1. I now want to make the nonstandard move of asking whether addiction could induce irrational *desires*, more specifically, irrational time preferences. Earlier I argued that a given rate of time discounting cannot in itself be seen as rational or irrational. I also suggested, however, that behavior induced by a momentary heightening of that rate is sufficiently similar to other forms of behavior that we would unambiguously characterize as irrational so as to merit the same label. With respect to addiction, Gary Becker writes, "A habit may be raised into an addiction by exposure to the habit itself. Certain habits, like drug use and heavy drinking, may reduce the attention to future consequences—there is no reason to assume discount rates on the future are just given and fixed."[67] In Becker's mind, this effect does not detract from the rationality of the addict. In my view, it does.

Choosing to Become an Addict

The question of whether addicts are irrational (discussed above) must be sharply distinguished from the question of whether it is irrational to *become* an addict. The latter issue can be broken down in three questions:

• Could it be rational to do *x* when (unbeknownst to the agent) *x* may or will induce addiction?
• Could it be rational to do *x* when the agent knows that *x will* induce addiction?
• Could it be rational to do *x* when the agent knows that *x may* induce addiction?

The first question corresponds to the "primrose path" theory of addiction proposed by Richard Herrnstein and Drazen Prelec, the second to the model of rational addiction developed by Gary Becker and Kevin Murphy, and the third to the idea, discussed by Athanasios Orphanides and David Zervos, that people may get addicted as the result of a calculated gamble.[68] Before discussing the models, I want to make two general remarks that apply to all of them.

First, we may note that in each case a positive answer to a given question is compatible with the idea that addicts behave irrationally. For the primrose-path theory, there is nothing irrational in embarking on a path that will lead to irrationality if the agent could not rationally anticipate that outcome. For the rational-addiction theory and the calculated-gamble theory, the suboptimalities induced by the irrational behavior of addicts could simply enter into the costs of addiction, on a par with physical or financial costs. On the rational-addiction theory, these costs would be incurred with certainty; on the calculated-gamble theory, they would be incurred only if the individual turns out to be an "addictive type."

Second, none of the models has anything to say about relapse. Herrnstein and Prelec's model explicitly presupposes a naive user, but you can be naive only once. Becker and Murphy's model can deal with relapse in the same way as it deals with the decision to start consuming in the first place, namely as a response to a life crisis or trauma (divorce or military service). Yet this approach suffers from the flaw of equating relapse and readdiction (see section 3.3). Orphanides and Zervos's model, like Herrnstein and Prelec's model, is simply inconsistent with relapse. If a person decides to start consuming, turns out to be an addictive type, and then manages to quit, one cannot explain relapse by stipulating that the person embarks on a new calculated gamble.

Herrnstein and Prelec view addictive behavior as a consequence of "internalities," that is, the tendency of consumption choices at one point in time to affect the welfare derived from consumption choices at a later point in time.[69] If this impact is negative and the consumer ignores it, he can be trapped into making a suboptimal choice.[70] A cigarette smoker, for instance, may not notice that by smoking a cigarette at 9:15 A.M., he reduces the pleasure he gets from smoking a cigarette at 9:30 A.M. At any given point, smoking may dominate nonsmoking in the smoker's mind even though he would derive greater total benefits from smoking by pacing himself. By the time he discovers that he is behaving suboptimally, it may be too late to cut down. Given the costs of withdrawal, smoking may then be his best option.

In Herrnstein's terminology, the smoker is *meliorating* rather than *maximizing*. To the extent that maximizing is seen as a hallmark of rationality, his addiction is irrational. Yet to the extent that the tendency to meliorate is a hardwired feature of the organism, the claim that it is irrational may seem unwarranted: here too "ought" implies "can." I incline, nevertheless, to view it as irrational. The smoker has available to him all the information he needs to form the correct belief about the internalities. And in fact, many people do form the belief after a while. Failure to do so is a form of belief irrationality. Yet much hinges on the clause "after a while." If the smoker gets addicted so fast that he does not have the time to develop the information he would need to understand the internality mechanism, he is subject to bad luck rather than to irrationality. This being said, in view of the current amount of publicity about the effects of drug use, it is unlikely that a beginning smoker would have no idea about the danger of addiction. The primrose path is a model of a naive addict who simply may not exist any more—or of a self-deceiving addict who is motivated to ignore the lessons from experience.

Becker and Murphy propose a theory that is at the opposite extreme from the primrose-path theory. On the rational-addiction theory, the beginning user is fully aware of the negative consequences of addiction. Moreover, he knows with certainty the level at which his consumption will eventually stabilize. Yet although the user does not suffer any cognitive deficiency, he is subject to what one might call a motivational deficiency, namely a positive rate of time discounting. Very simply put and with many technical details omitted, Becker and Murphy view addiction as a form of rational self-medication in which (the discounted value of) the future cost of addiction counts for less than the current pleasure from consumption. As mentioned above, the medication is a response to some traumatic event, in the light of which the short-term alleviation of misery provided by the drug more than offsets the (discounted) misery expected to follow as the result of drug taking. Although the model is formally consistent and may in some cases yield an accurate explanation of why people start taking drugs, the full-information assumption is too unrealistic to make the theory of any interest outside special cases.

An intermediate case between full information and no information is that of the calculated gamble. The potential consumer knows that he might become an addict but also that he might be able to consume the drug recreationally with no serious negative effects. (As mentioned above, we may include a reduced capacity to make rational decisions among these effects.) In this case we may ask, first, what a rational person should do to find out whether he is a "vulnerable" type or an "immune" type and, second, whether people actually behave in this way before they begin to consume potentially addictive drugs. As little is known about the second issue, I shall have to rely on casual observation.

To find about one's type, one should first gather information about the proportion of people who try a certain drug and then go on to get hooked. Among those who experiment with intravenous cocaine, for instance, one third don't like it the first time, one third try it again without developing any problems, and one third try it again and go on to ruin their lives through lost jobs, lost families, legal troubles, lost savings, and so on.[71] Next one might try to get more personalized information about oneself, by consulting doctors, seeking information about genetic predispositions, and so on. Finally one might try to experiment with the drug to decide whether one is vulnerable. I now consider this case in more detail.

In the model proposed by Orphanides and Zervos, individuals start out with initial beliefs about how likely they are to be vulnerable. These beliefs may be partly formed by information of the kinds just mentioned but also by government warnings, advertising, interaction with peers, etc. From these beliefs, some individuals may decide to abstain altogether from the drug. Others may decide that it is worth the risk to find out whether they are vulnerable or safe. Even though they know that they might turn out to be vulnerable and become addicted, the expected utility of experimenting exceeds that of abstaining. Because the negative side effects of addiction occur stochastically (a crucial assumption in the model), a vulnerable individual might suffer the bad luck of not discovering his type until it is too late, that is, until a point when his optimal path is continued consumption as an addict. Other vulnerable types might experience the side effects earlier, and thus be able to quit. In addition to these never-users, addicted users, and ex-users, there are some who succeed in becoming controlled casual users.

In Orphanides and Zervos's model, people never choose to become addicted, as they do in Becker and Murphy's model. Instead, individuals who aim at controlled use take the risk of becoming addicted. Their model thus captures the involuntary aspect of addiction that is central in real-life cases. In other respects, the model is less satisfactory. The idea that addiction is the result of a calculated gamble has no direct confirmation in any empirical studies of addiction known to me.[72] Among the numerous paths to addiction, calculated gambles must be one of the rarest. To the extent that this mechanism operates, I believe that different degrees of risk aversion are as important as different initial beliefs about one's type. Also, the model gives too much importance to experimentation as a source of belief updating and too little importance to other sources of information. If people are as rational as the model makes them out to be, they would invest very heavily in general and specific information about the dangers of addiction before deciding whether to experiment. These are, after all, activities that could destroy their lives. As a matter of fact, however, people do not seem to gather extensive medical information before embarking on an addictive career.[73]

The model also assumes an unrealistic degree of accuracy in people's beliefs about the harms of addiction. This is a question not of assessing the likelihood of this or that harmful effect being produced but of assessing how bad *addiction will feel* if it occurs. As argued by Loewenstein, people tend systematically to underestimate the impact of future visceral experiences.[74] Also, "people's risk behaviors are . . . imperfect indicators of the risks that they believe themselves to be taking. For example, investors may not realize that they are boarding an emotional rollercoaster when they assign half of their pension to an equity fund. Nor is there any guarantee that the impact of acknowledged consequences will be perceived accurately."[75] Similarly, incipient addicts may not be able anticipate the subjective impact of correctly anticipated objective consequences.

Addiction and Self-Control

The simplest recipe for quitting—"Just do it!"—is often simplistic. In the short run, withdrawal symptoms and the tendency to hyperbolic discounting may be enough to break down the resolve to quit. In the long run,

a series of virtually unsurmountable neurobiological hurdles are erected in the path of drug addicts wishing to stay abstinent—(1) by virtue of their prior chronic drug use, the pleasure/reward circuits of their brains have been forever changed so that they now possess heightened vulnerability to addicted drugs; (2) this heightened vulnerability includes a heightened cross-vulnerability to other drugs which activate the pleasure/reward circuits of the brain, even drugs to which the addict may never have been exposed; (3) this heightened vulnerability can be triggered not only by drugs, but by stressors and environmental cues previously associated with drug-taking.[76]

In addition, memories of drug euphoria can trigger cravings and relapse in both the short run and the long run. For many addicts, quitting is an obstacle course that is simply too difficult to tackle by sheer strength of will. Instead, addicts use indirect strategies of various kinds to resist temptation. Elsewhere, I have referred to these procedures as "imperfect rationality."[77]

In general, these indirect strategies can be either cognitive or behavioral. The former fall in one of two subcategories: bunching and sophisticated choice. The latter takes the form of precommitment, i.e., of manipulating the environment so as to make it more difficult, costly, or even impossible to consume the addictive substance. In the case of addiction, bunching and pre-commitment appear to be more promising than sophistication, which may actually be counterproductive.

First consider *bunching*. As George Ainslie has shown, a person who is subject to hyperbolic discounting may bootstrap himself out of addiction by viewing each relapse as a predictor of future relapses.[78] In this perspective, the choice is not between, say, drinking today and not drinking today, but between drinking today and on all later occasions and not drinking either today or on any later occasion. The addict forms a "private rule" that protects him against temptation. Whether or not one views this bunching strategy as relying on rational beliefs or rather on a form of magical thinking,[79] there is no doubt that it can be an effective way of overcoming temptation. In the case of addiction, it is perhaps more plausible as a strategy of relapse prevention than as a strategy of quitting. For a person who is still in the grip of his addiction, the craving for the drug may be so strong that the short-term reward dominates *at all times*, a situation that corresponds to an upward shift of curve I in figure 5.2 above. Also, Ole-Jørgen Skog has shown that if the number of future periods bunched together is small enough, an addict may form a resolution to quit only to find that it dissolves when the moment of choice approaches, which thus reproduces the problem of time inconsistency that motivated the bunching in the first place.[80]

Next consider *sophisticated choice*. In this cognitive strategy, those who are subject to hyperbolic discounting may try to make the best out of the situation by anticipating their future discounting. Yet in the case of addiction, this sophisticated strategy may actually make things worse. As Ted O'Donoghue and Matthew Rabin observe, "Knowing about future self-control problems can lead you to give in to them today, because you realize you will give in to them tomorrow."[81] The idea is confirmed by clinical evidence from treating addicts, which suggests that they have often fatalistic attitudes: "Since I know I'm going to relapse sooner or later, I might as well begin today."[82]

Finally consider *precommitment strategies*. Whereas bunching and sophisticated choice are responses to hyperbolic discounting, precommitment behavior is a response to the whole range of obstacles that face the addict who is trying to quit, and thus takes a correspondingly large variety of forms.[83]

First, the addict may place himself in a situation in which the addictive substance is physically unavailable. In some cases, it may be possible to make the addictive substance physically unavailable, at least for a while. This strategy may be combined with the imposition or utilization of delays. If I know I shall want to drink in the evening but that liquor stores will be closed, not keeping liquor in the house will carry me over the dangerous period until next morning, when the stores are open but I know I shall not want to drink.

Second, the addict may enlist other people as agents to protect him against himself. The first instance of this strategy I have come across is in a sworn and witnessed statement made by one James Chalmers of New Jersey in 1795: "Whereas, the subscriber, through the pernicious habit of drinking, has greatly hurt himself in purse and person, and rendered himself odious to all his acquaintances and finds that there is no possibility of breaking off from the said practice *but through the impossibility to find liquor*, he therefore begs and prays that no person will sell him for money, or on trust, any sort of spirituous liquor."[84]

Third, he may overcome problems of hyperbolic discounting by creating a delay between the time of making the decision to consume and the time at which the substance becomes available. In terms of figure 5.2 above, any delay greater than the interval between time 1 and t^* will be sufficient to ensure that by the time he is in a position to choose, he will make the "right" choice.

Fourth, the agent may overcome temptation by imposing costs on himself, i.e., by inducing a downward shift of curve I in figure 5.2. Thomas Schelling provides a vivid example:

In a cocaine addiction center in Denver, patients are offered an opportunity to submit to extortion. They may write a self-incriminating letter, preferably a letter confessing their drug addiction, deposit the letter with the clinic, and submit to a randomized schedule of laboratory tests. If the laboratory finds evidence of cocaine use, the clinic sends the letter to the addressee. An example is a physician who addresses a letter to the State Board of Medical Examiners confessing that he has administered cocaine to himself in violation of the laws of Colorado and requests that his license to practice be revoked.[85]

Fifth, the addict may act to modify his preferences, by hypnosis, aversion therapy, and cue-extinction techniques. A survey of the use of hypnosis to curb smoking, obesity, substance abuse, and alcoholism found very modest success rates.[86] Aversion therapy, using classical conditioning principles to get the addict to associate the drug with nausea or electrical shocks, also has had quite limited success.[87] Whereas aversion therapy aims at establishing a negative conditioned response to drugs, cue extinction aims at eliminating positive responses. The addict has to be brought or to bring himself into the environments or situations traditionally associated with consumption and then to be prevented or to prevent himself from consuming. As the connection is broken, the cue-dependent cravings will fade after a while.[88] As shown by Goldstein's story about the smoker who had forgotten that smoking was associated with going to the beach (section 2.3), the process must be systematic and cover all the situations habitually associated with the drug.

Finally, an alternative to cue extinction is cue avoidance, in which one manipulates the environment rather than the addict's reactions to it. As noted in note 42 to chapter 4, it has been claimed both that Alcoholics Anonymous adopts the strategy of cue extinction and that it uses the strategy of cue avoidance. As these strategies are mutually exclusive, both claims cannot be right.

Summary

The relation between addiction and choice is intimate and complex. Addiction arises as the result of voluntary choices; once established, it undermines the capacity to choose or at least to make rational choices; and it can be overcome only by (imperfectly) rational choice. Addictive cravings themselves are not the object of choice. Whether (like some emotions) they arise suddenly in the mind from perception or cognition or (like other emotions) are constant preoccupations that dominate all other concerns, cravings are involuntary. On some occasions, they may even be irresistible. More frequently, cravings compete with other motivations and rewards. In George Ainslie's phrase, they operate in the same marketplace. They can thus be overcome by setting up appropriate incentive systems. Alternatively, the addict can try to short-circuit the problem by avoiding the circumstances in which cravings are triggered or by making sure he has no means of satisfying them.

6　　　Conclusion

Many emotions and addictions involve "strong feelings," characterized by physical arousal and negative
or positive affect. They share these features with other
states of the organism, such as pain or sexual arousal.
As George Loewenstein has argued, these visceral
states have many similar effects on cognition and
behavior. Intense pain, intense shame, intense sexual
arousal, and intense craving for cocaine have in common a capacity to derail the agent from his normal
mode of functioning and to induce behaviors that go
against what external observers and the agent himself,
before and after the visceral experience, would deem
to be in his best interest.

Some visceral states are essentially independent of,
and impermeable to, external or internal influences.
Nobody, to my knowledge, has attempted to argue that
pain is a "social construction." George Ainslie's claim
that pain is *chosen* because of the short-term reward it
offers to the agent is intrinsically implausible and (what
is more important) not supported by any direct evidence. The need to relieve a full bladder is similarly
independent of culture and choice. Although these vis-

ceral disturbances can affect cognition and behavior, their origin is entirely physical. This statement does not imply that their impact on cognition and behavior is mind-independent. The fact that some people refuse to talk under severe torture shows that the need to relieve intense pain need not be irresistible. The driver who feels an overwhelming drowsiness coming over him may be able to stay awake by pinching himself in the arm, thus using one visceral factor to counteract another. Visceral factors do not affect the capacity for purposive behavior in the manner of Alzheimer's disease, which acts on the core of the mind, not merely on its periphery. These are metaphors, but the contrast should be clear.

This subset of visceral factors must be distinguished from those shaped in part by culture and choice, namely emotions and the states induced by addictive substances. By and large (but see section 2.3 for exceptions), all emotions involve physiological arousal and either positive or negative valence. Addictive substances also modify the physiological state of the organism in a number of ways, by what I called their "primary nonhedonic effects" (section 3.4). In addition, there is a hedonic impact, which is positive during consumption and negative during abstinence. The hedonic and nonhedonic effects jointly influence the state of *craving*, which is the central explanatory variable in the behavioral study of addiction and its consequences. Although the states of euphoria or dysphoria associated with consumption or abstinence are not themselves intentional, they can induce a craving for the euphoria-inducing or dysphoria-alleviating substance.

Euphoric or dysphoric states associated with emotion are, by and large, triggered by beliefs. Euphoric or dysphoric states associated with addiction are, by and large, triggered by the injection of a chemical substance and by its disappearance from the body. Although extremely different in origin, the phenomenology of the states can be quite similar. As I mentioned in chapter 1, the subjective effects of amphetamine and of love are quite similar—not only the hedonic aspects but nonhedonic aspects as well, such as reduced need for sleep or food. The difference is that the person who is in love can only think about one thing, whereas amphetamines can enhance concentration on any activity. Sartre wrote *Critique de la raison dialectique* under its influence, and many students have taken it to write their term essays.

Beliefs can also have a role in the etiology of addictive states. Most obviously, beliefs matter for craving. A patient who has received morphine in the hospital and feels the typical withdrawal symptoms upon release will not crave the drug if he is unaware that his suffering is caused by drug abstinence and can be relieved by drug use.[1] Beliefs can also matter for the state of dysphoria that generates a craving. Although I am unaware of systematic studies on the subject, casual observation and introspection suggest that when the agent believes that a substance is unavailable, or that its use will be subject to immediate sanctioning, the craving subsides. In addition to Goldstein's skier example, cited in section 3.3, one may cite the fact that some heavy smokers have little difficulty going without cigarettes on transatlantic flights if smoking is forbidden, yet they feel intense craving once they approach an area where they can smoke.[2]

Whatever the importance of belief-dependent cravings, cue dependence is a very central and well-documented mechanism. By the mechanism of conditioned learning, addicts may experience euphoria, dysphoria, and craving at the mere sight or smell of an environment associated with their consumption. An ex-addict can relapse simply by watching a TV program about addiction.[3] The same mechanism—sensory cues invested with significance through associative learning—can also trigger emotion. As LeDoux has shown, conditioned stimuli may even trigger emotions such as fear when there is no conscious memory of the original event that established the association. In fact, very traumatic events may have the dual effect of creating strong emotional or implicit memories that can recreate the emotion under the appropriate circumstances *and* of preventing the formation of conscious or explicit memories.[4] If this hypothesis is verified, Freud will have been proved wrong: lack of memory about traumatic events cannot be due to repression if the memory has not been formed in the first place.

The causal origin of the link between perception and emotion may be found in evolution rather than in associative learning. A snakelike shape on one's path may trigger an emotion of fear and a behavioral response of freezing because this is what evolution has programmed to happen. Cue-dependent cravings, by contrast, can only arise through learning. Although the mechanism of associative learning is a result of natural selection and associative learning may induce cue-dependent cravings, it is unimaginable that natural selection could induce craving at the sight or smell of alcohol in a person who had never tasted it. Cravings, unlike emotions, are artificial phenomena. For one thing, animal addiction does not occur spontaneously in the wild, and in some human groups, addiction does not exist. For another, evolution has not produced a specialized neurophysiological machinery for responding to addictive substances. Instead, addiction occurs when and because a chemical substance happens to fit into a brain reward system that evolved to ensure that the organism is motivated to satisfy basic needs of food, drink, and sex.

From a conceptual point of view, it is important to emphasize that emotions can be triggered by perceptions in which no cognitive content (in the form of propositional beliefs) is involved. In addition to fear and perhaps a few other very basic emotions, the aesthetic emotions also illustrate this idea. This having been said, the more complex emotions are mostly triggered by beliefs rather than by perception. With cravings, it is the other way around: whereas cue dependence is a massively important mechanism, belief dependence is probably marginal. This discussion is summarized in table 6.1, with the most prominent cases starred.

This typology presupposes that the emotion or craving is initially absent and then suddenly triggered by some external event. In the terminology of section 2.3 above, such states are characterized by "sudden onset," "unbidden occurrence," and "brief duration." Yet *strong feelings are not necessarily transient.* As we also saw in section 2.3, emotions such as love or wrath (the emotional desire for revenge) can persist for years or decades unless or until they are satisfied. An emotion can serve as the organizing principle of a life. Some addicts too are in a more or less constant state of crav-

Table 6.1
Belief dependence and cue dependence in emotions versus cravings

Trigger	Emotions triggered	Cravings triggered
Cognition	Complex emotions*	Belief-dependent cravings
Perception	Fear, aesthetic emotions	Cue-dependent cravings*

* = central case

ing. The life of the alcoholic, the heroin addict, or the compulsive gambler is organized around getting to the next drink, the next fix, or a source of gambling funds. Citing Herbert Fingarette and Francis Seeburger, Gary Watson refers to this form of addiction as "existential dependence."[5]

Beliefs enter, more or less prominently, among the causes of emotions and cravings. Conversely, strong feelings can affect cognition, by clouding or distorting it. The clouding effect may occur simply because it is hard to think rationally under the influence of visceral feelings, which may distract from the long trains of thought often required. Very intense feelings also have the capacity for inducing a disregard of alternatives to the option they favor and of its long-term consequences. The urge to strike back in anger or the craving for cocaine may be so strong that other considerations simply do not present themselves to the mind of the agent, or do so in a way that reduces their motivational power. The philosophically controversial question of whether the clouding effect can be so strong as to make the desire literally irresistible is not very important in practice. It is uncontroversial that emotions and cravings can induce an agent to disregard alternatives and consequences much more than he would under other circumstances.

With regard to the emotions, various writers argue that the shrinking of the cognitive horizon is actually beneficial, and may have been selected for by natural evolution. The need to respond to danger may be so urgent that careful and time-consuming consideration of alternatives and consequences might defeat its purpose. This argument fails on a number of counts. First, saying that "in responding first with its most-likely-to-succeed behavior, the brain buys time . . . is not to say that the brain responds automatically for the purpose of buying time. The automatic responses came first, in the evolutionary sense, and cannot exist for the purpose of serving responses that came later."[6] Second, emotions that arise in situations where buying time is inessential may also cloud belief formation—shame is an example. Third, the fact that addictive cravings as well as other visceral feelings such as pain can have the same effect suggests that emotional truncation of cognition can be explained more parsimoniously by its proximate causes than by its evolutionary origins.

The distorting effect occurs when the belief is harnessed to the desire. Smokers welcome theories that justify their behavior by asserting that the craving to smoke is irresistible. The relapsing ex-alcoholic is motivated to believe in the theory of Alcoholics Anonymous according to which the first drink inevitably turns into a binge. Emotions too motivate the agent to seek out justifications for the behaviors they induce. As Seneca said, "Reason wishes the decision that it gives to be just; anger wishes to have the decision which it has given seem the just decision."[7] Love, according to Stendhal's theory of crystallization, manages to find all sorts of wonderful qualities in the object of love to justify a feeling that originally had no other root than the belief that the other person might love oneself. By virtue of the high levels of arousal and valence they induce, emotions and cravings are among the most powerful sources of denial, self-deception, and rationalization in human life.

Addicts get their ideas about the nature of addiction and relapse from their environment. In addition to causal beliefs, the environment also provides them with norms and values. Such beliefs, norms, and values differ across and within societies. In addition to the examples discussed in section 4.3, one can use eating disorders to illustrate this idea.

The ordinary overweight person in the stylized representation of figure 6.1 will often be found in cultures and subcultures less concerned with body weight and slimness than is the case among professionals in contemporary Western societies. For many people in the past, for instance, the prospect of gaining weight as they grew older was seen as normal and (at least for men) even desirable. As values change and as people acquire ever-more complex causal beliefs about the relation among food intake, weight, and health, new patterns of weight change emerge. In addition to the serious eating disturbances of anorexia nervosa and bulimia, there are numerous off-on dieters whose weight pattern somewhat resembles that of bulimics. Charting drinking patterns before and after the "discovery of alcoholism" would probably yield qualitatively similar results. As in the case of eating disorders, the key explanatory vari-

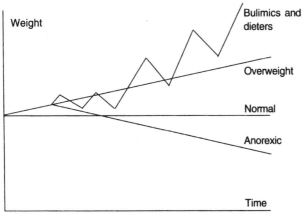

Figure 6.1
Eating disorders.

able is the emergence of *ambivalence*, caused by the conflict between the craving to consume and the social disapproval of consumption.

In the case of emotions, causal beliefs do not matter
very much. Although there is evidence that both
occurrent episodes of anger[8] and chronic irascibility[9]
increase the risk of coronary heart disease, this evidence
has not yet hardened into popular beliefs that might
induce people to try to control their emotions. If those
beliefs did emerge, they might have to confront evidence to the effect that *repressing* emotions may also
have bad health effects, by causing hypertension[10] and
worsening the prognosis for cancer patients.[11] By and
large, beliefs of this kind are not an integral part of our
attitudes toward the emotions, as beliefs about the bad-
health consequences of smoking are part of our attitude
toward cigarette addiction.

By contrast, occurrent emotions as well as emotional dispositions are very much the subject of normative assessments. Again, there is much cultural variation. A society that does not explicitly label and conceptualize a given emotion cannot harbor positive or negative attitudes toward it either. Also, even if the emotion is acknowledged as such, normative attitudes toward it may vary a great deal. What we would view as the overbearing and intolerable pride of Renaissance kings or princes was accepted as their due at the time. Whereas we tend to condemn an unbridled passion for revenge, other societies have condemned those who did not feel it on the appropriate occasions. In one society, people may feel and show contempt for disfigured or obese individuals, whereas in another that attitude itself would be met with contempt.

Cultural variations in attitudes toward emotions and cravings may have their source in the different valuations of self-control. According to one set of norms, people approve most highly of those who are able to control their urges and cravings but nevertheless disapprove less of those who do not try to control themselves than of those who try and fail. In other norm systems, the second-ranked group might instead be at the top or at the bottom of the value hierarchy. As I am unaware of any systematic studies of the subject, these remarks are speculative and nonspecific. What seems clear is that in the phenomenology of addiction and emotion, self-control as a source of esteem and self-esteem have an important place. For some alcoholics, the most painful cause of shame and guilt is that by drinking they are doing harm to themselves and their families. For others, it is that they are showing themselves to be incapable of carrying out their decision to quit. Irascible individuals might also be viewed—by themselves and others—in either perspective. I conjecture that comparative studies would show these attitudes to vary systematically across societies, not merely idiosyncratically across individuals.

Yet in all societies it is probably recognized that some emotions and cravings can be so self-destructive in their consequences that self-control to keep them in check is to be valued. While subject to emotions and cravings, as well as to social norms and values directed toward these feelings, people are also capable of thinking and acting rationally. Although this capacity can be subverted by the feelings, it can also be used to resist them. The hardest thing is to resist a strong feeling at the moment it arises. In the case of anger (see figure 2.1 above), one may not be aware of the emotion until it is too late. In the middle of a cocaine binge, prior resolutions of self-control no longer have the power to motivate, and costs of the behavior are largely ignored.

An alternative to "instant self-control" is to adopt one of several indirect strategies. On the one hand, the agent can take as given the tendency or disposition to feel cravings or emotions in a given environment and try to adjust strategically to the latter, either by avoiding situations that might trigger the desire or by removing the means of satisfying it. Some addicts learn to avoid environments associated with their earlier drug taking, whereas others give or throw away the key that would give them access to the drug they want to avoid. Ulysses could have put wax in his own ears so that he would not hear the song of the Sirens, but chose instead to tie himself to the mast so that he was physically unable to give in to the emotion it produced.

On the other hand, the agent may try to modify the disposition itself, so that he can move freely among dangers and temptations without giving them a second thought. An addict may rid himself of cue-dependent cravings by a process of systematic desensitization, exposing himself to the cues without subsequent consumption until the association has been broken. The person who wants to rid himself of a tendency to feel irrational guilt can engage in meditation or therapy for that purpose.

Because of the artificial and limited nature of addiction, these self-control strategies are more likely to succeed in the case of cravings than in the case of emotions. Short of shying away from all contact with other people, it would be impossible for an irascible person to avoid all occasions for anger or to prevent himself from acting on his anger on all occasions he might feel it. By contrast, the set of environments and cues associated with drug taking is often small enough to make complete avoidance possible.

To the extent that emotional dispositions are established by associative learning, as with conditioned fear reactions or phobias, it is also possible to unlearn them by desensitization. Yet the subset of emotions of which this is true is relatively small. Most emotional dispositions cannot be eliminated by producing the occasions on which they tend to occur and then refraining from acting on them. To my knowledge, nothing suggests, for instance, that one could become less irascible by suppressing the behavioral manifestations of anger. By contrast, because associative learning is central in the etiology of cravings, desensitization is a more promising strategy of self-control in this case.

In this chapter, and in the book as a whole, I have tried to bring out similarities as well as differences between emotion and addiction. Both phenomena arise in the intersection of neurobiology, culture, and choice. Although both have a firm basis in neuropsychological mechanisms, they are also malleable to some extent by the choices of the agent and by the beliefs, norms, and values of his environment. At the same time, the arousal and hedonic valence that characterize strong emotions and cravings are also capable of undermining cognition, choice, and rationality.

These common features must be seen against the background of two important differences. Emotions are natural and universal. Without asserting that there are some emotions that are found in all societies, I can safely say that all societies feature some emotions. Addiction is artificial and nonuniversal, an accident of the interaction between the brain reward machinery that evolved for other purposes and certain chemical substances. At the same time, emotions are much more belief-dependent than addictive cravings and drug-induced states. Because social life is embedded in an extraordinarily dense network of beliefs, emotions are central to all human activities. In comparison, the role of cognition and even perception in addiction is sharply limited.

Yet some mysteries remain. Why are love and amphetamine, so different in their causes, so similar in their effects? How do guilt and shame from drug use interact with the dysphoria induced by withdrawal? Why do we sometimes have the impression that a person is addicted to the emotion of righteous indignation, seeking out all occasions that will produce it? Beneath the differences, there may be further similarities that we do not yet understand.

Notes

Chapter 1

1. Loewenstein (1996, 1998).

2. Liebowitz (1983), pp. 92–103.

3. Tennov (1979).

4. See for instance the many vivid descriptions in Stendhal (1980) and Tennov (1979).

5. Lewis (1992), p. 78

6. Liebowitz (1983), pp. 91–95.

7. Peele and Brodsky (1991).

8. See, for instance, the discussion of the analogous extension of the concept of "capital" in Elster (1997). The principle that everything is a little bit like everything else might be called the first law of pseudoscience. The second law is that everything is causally connected to everything else, an idea that induces a reluctance to analytical modeling, which inevitably abstracts from some causally relevant features of the situation in order to understand the role of the most important ones.

9. Thompson (1992), p. 961.

10. See Gardner and David (1998) for a striking comparison between animal and human crack addiction. The claim is not that human addicts and addicted rats literally engage in the same behavior, but rather that in their efforts to obtain the drug, both seem to

display the same disregard for all other considerations. See also section 5.3 below.

11. A case of possible animal ambivalence is discussed by Spealman (1979), who found that "squirrel monkeys self-administered cocaine by pressing a lever while under a variable-interval schedule of reinforcement. At the same time, they terminated the availability of self-administered cocaine by pressing a second lever while under a fixed-interval schedule of reinforcement." See also Altman et al. (1996), p. 291.

Chapter 2

1. Montaigne (1991), p. 975.

2. Hume (1960), pp. 375–376, treats envy as a mere interpersonal contrast effect, that is, as analogous to what we experience when we compare our present state with an earlier and happier one (see also Elster and Loewenstein 1992). This sanitized conception of envy is of little help in explaining the destructive virulence of the emotion.

3. Montaigne (1991), p. 9.

4. The most baffling case is that of Dostoyevsky. Some of the characters in his novels are both plausible and opaque; their behavior is neither "out of character" nor "in character."

5. Wilson (1988), pp. 30, 280.

6. "Men become calm when they have spent their anger on someone else. This happened in the case of Ergophilus: though the people were more irritated against him than against Callisthenes, they acquitted him because they had condemned Callisthenes to death the day before" (Aristotle, *Rhetoric* 1380b, 11–13). In trials of collaborators in German-occupied countries after World War II, those who were tried later generally received milder sentences even when the crimes were similar (Elster 1998f).

7. See Roth (1995) for a survey.

8. See Elster (1998a) for some suggestions.

9. Cameron (1995).

10. Loewenstein (1996); Loewenstein and Schkade (1998).

11. LeDoux (1996). For other studies of fear, see Marks (1987) and Gray (1991).

12. De Waal (1996), p. 110.

13. Vollmer (1977).

14. Descartes, *Les passions de l'âme*, art. 201.

15. In the following, I include "nonundeserved" under the heading of "deserved." Thus when someone wins a big prize in the lottery, I shall say that it is deserved, somewhat contrary to ordinary usage.

16. Elster and Loewenstein (1992) argue that the same is true for good or bad future events.

17. Stendhal (1980), Tennov (1979). La Rochefoucauld, *Maxims*, no. 32; Proust (1954), vol. 1, p. 365.

18. For two opposed views, see Walton (1990) and Yanal (1994).

19. The second, third, and fourth features are taken from Ekman (1992a). In discussing the other features, I draw heavily on the outstanding synthetic exposition by Frijda (1986).

20. Budd (1995), p. 136.

21. For direct brain stimulation, see Brothers (1995), p. 1111, citing Gloor (1986), p. 164. For chemical stimulation, see Servan-Schreiber and Perlstein (1997).

22. Ekman (1992a), p. 185.

23. Frijda (1986), pp. 43–45, 91, 241.

24. Montaigne (1991), p. 1154; see also Ekman (1992b), p. 47.

25. Cited after Sellier (1991), p. 395, n. 1.

26. Ekman (1992a), p. 185.

27. Tennov (1979), p. 142.

28. Djilas (1958), pp. 86, 105, 106, 107.

29. LeDoux (1996), p. 163–165.

30. One special case is related to the "cocktail party phenomenon." At a cocktail party, we usually screen out background noise to focus on what our interlocutor is saying. Yet if our own name is mentioned, we immediately pick it up. Similarly, if the name of a longstanding enemy is mentioned in a background conversation, it is conceivable that we start reacting emotionally before our cortex can decide whether the full propositional context justifies anger.

31. This is a purely speculative assertion. As far as I know, there is no neurophysiological evidence of distinct high-road and low-road pathways in the generation of anger. Yet at the phenomenological level, there is abundant evidence that people sometimes lash out in anger before they have time to decide whether their aggression is justified.

32. Stendhal (1980), p. 279.

33. See for instance Gordon (1987).

34. Budd (1995), p. 149.

35. Frijda (1986), chap. 2, has a full survey.

36. Levenson (1992), p. 26.

37. Gordon (1987), p. 77.

38. Frijda (1986), p. 173.

39. Frijda (1986), p. 12.

40. Ekman (1992b).

41. Carroll (1996), p. 131.

42. Hume (1960), p. 367.

43. Fry (1921), p. 13; also Budd (1995), p. 77.

44. Tesser (1991). Hume (1960, p. 278) was wrong, therefore, when he asserted, "To excite any passion, and at the same time raise an equal share of its antagonist, is immediately to undo what was done, and must leave the mind at last perfectly calm and indifferent." The fallacy is to identify "calm" and "indifferent." The first refers to absence of arousal, the second to absence of net pleasure or pain.

45. Panksepp (1993), p. 90.

46. Panksepp (1993), p. 90.

47. There are two aspects of this feedback loop. On the one hand, "once the amygdala is activated, it is able to influence the cortical areas that are processing the stimuli that are activating it. . . . This might be very important in directing attention to emotionally relevant stimuli by keeping the short-term object buffer [a memory-storage mechanism] focused on the stimuli to which the amygdala is assigning significance" (LeDoux 1996, pp. 284–285). This aspect of the feedback is obviously adaptive. On the other hand, "the con-

nections from the cortical areas to the amygdala are far weaker than the connections from the amygdala to the cortex. This may explain why it is so easy for emotional information to invade our conscious thought, but so hard for us to gain conscious control over our emotions" (LeDoux 1996, p. 265). Here LeDoux seems to suggest a non-adaptive aspect of the feedback. This seems intuitively right: the emotions can alert us to the fact that something important is going on, but they can also get out of hand and make it harder for us to deal efficiently with the problem.

48. From LeDoux (1993), p. 112.

49. LeDoux (1996), pp. 126–127; see also LeDoux (1995), pp. 1049–1050.

50. Frijda (1986), p. 117; see also p. 155, where he discusses the view that the negative side effects of epinephrine secretion might actually outweigh the beneficial effects.

51. Frijda (1986), p. 115.

52. Frijda (1986), p. 115.

53. Frank (1988) offers a sustained argument to this effect. Although he emphasizes *indignation* (moral outrage at being unfairly treated) rather than *anger* per se (which can also be triggered by mere wish frustration), I do not believe the distinction is crucially important. As shown by Linda Babcock, George Loewenstein, and their coworkers (Loewenstein et al. 1993, Babcock et al. 1995, Babcock and Loewenstein 1997), the conceptions of fairness that underlie the indignation may themselves be generated by self-interest.

Chapter 3

1. *Pensées* (ed. Sellier), no. 139.

2. Goldstein (1994), p. 83.

3. Simon (1997), p. 154.

4. Robinson and Berridge (1993), p. 254.

5. Schmitz, Schneider, and Jarvik (1997), pp. 281–283.

6. Edwards et al. (1994), p. 137. A Norwegian policy experiment had similar results.

7. Peele (1985), p. 25.

8. Peele (1985), p. 99. See below for some comments on this criticism.

9. Goldstein (1994), pp. 3–5 and passim.

10. Marks (1990).

11. Hoebel (forthcoming).

12. Thus in *DSM* IV (American Psychiatric Association 1994, p. 181) substance dependence is identified as the copresence of any three of seven defining features.

13. See for instances Gardner (1997), p. 68.

14. Robinson and Berridge (1993), pp. 266–267.

15. Robinson and Berridge (1993), p. 261.

16. Robinson and Berridge (1993), p. 271.

17. Robinson and Berridge (1993), p. 271.

18. Satel (1992), pp. 176–177.

19. Gossop (1990) seems to conflate these two issues.

20. Schultz, Dayan, and Montague (1997).

21. See also Warburton (1990) and Klein (1993).

22. Steele and Josephs (1990), p. 928, citing Banaji and Steele (1989); italics in original.

23. Robinson and Berridge (1993), p. 275.

24. Lesieur (1984), p. 44.

25. Cues may also be internal or interoceptive. Thus for one patient, emotional distress triggers cocaine craving; for another, elation has the same effect (Margolin and Avants 1992, pp. 118–119).

26. Siegel, Krank, and Hinson (1988); O'Brien et al. (1992).

27. For an explanation of this difference, see Eikelboom and Stewart (1982). Childress et al. note, "Both drug-opposite and drug-like conditioned responses could put a patient at risk for drug use. He or she may be 'pushed' to seek relief from the discomfort of drug-opposite responses, or may be 'pulled' to seek the reward 'promised' by the drug" (1992, p. 59).

28. Siegel, Krank, and Hinson (1988), p. 89.

29. Goldstein (1994), p. 222.

30. Elster (1983; 1998e, chap. 1, sec. 6). In many cases of sour grapes, however, the adaptation tends to overshoot: rather than ceasing to desire the grapes, the fox actually thought them to be undesirable. The belief dependence of cravings does not have this property. While away from the lodge, the skier probably did not form a belief that cigarettes were aversive—he simply didn't give them a thought.

31. Steele and Josephs (1990), p. 921. By contrast, smoking actually *saves* public money. Smokers will be less of a burden on the health-care system in their old age—because fewer of them live to an old age (data by Kip Viscusi reported in Kluger 1996, p. 737).

32. Peck (1986), p. 462.

33. Bourgois (1995) offers a particularly vivid description.

34. Goldstein (1994), p. 188.

35. Bozarth (1990), p. 113; Seeburger (1993), p. 83.

36. Steele and Josephs (1990), p. 923.

37. Gardner and David (1998) suggest that this effect might be due to cross-tolerance rather than to disinhibition. Baumeister, Heath-erton, and Tice (1994, p. 205) assert that the issue remains open. Also, if smoking and drinking have regularly been associated in the past, alcohol might trigger relapse among smokers via cue-dependence (Ashton and Stepney 1982, p. 160). A fourth possibility is that "smokers may use the stimulant properties of nicotine to counter the depressant effects of alcohol" (Ashton and Stepney 1982, p. 108).

38. Weiss, Mirin, and Bartel (1994), p. 76.

39. Satel (1992), pp. 179–188.

40. Peck (1986), p. 464.

41. McKim (1991), p. 292; Doweiko (1996), p. 126.

42. Jellinek (1960), p. 38.

43. Schelling (1998) has a full discussion of the multiple ambiguities involved.

44. Peele (1985), p. 59.

45. Twerski (1990); Orford (1985), pp. 242–244.

46. Vaillant (1995), pp. 362–363.

47. Ainslie (1992).

48. Elster (1984).

49. Robinson and Berridge (1993), p. 252.

50. Elster (1998b).

51. Robinson and Berridge (1993); Schultz, Dayan, and Montague (1997); Wickelgren (1997).

52. For nicotine, see Schmitz, Schneider, and Jarvik (1997), p. 280.

53. Robinson and Berridge (1993), p. 175.

54. Goldstein (1994), p. 82. There is evidence, however, that this homeostatic model may be too simple. Rather than the consumption of a drug triggering an increase of dopamine release, which in turn triggers a compensatory dopamine-reducing mechanism, there may be two mechanisms that are triggered simultaneously, albeit with different temporal profiles. This "opponent-process theory" (Solomon and Corbit 1974) stipulates that "drug reinforcers arouse *both* positive (appetitive, pleasurable) and negative (aversive, dysphoric) hedonic processes in the brain, and that these processes oppose one another in a simple dynamic system. . . . The positive hedonic processes are hypothesized to be simple, stable, of short latency and duration, to follow the reinforcer closely, and to develop tolerance rapidly. The negative hedonic processes are hypothesized to be of longer latency and duration (thus, they build up strength and decay more slowly), and to be resistant to the development of tolerance" (Gardner 1997, p. 68). Even if this causal hypothesis proves to be correct, the observed changes will still correspond to the pattern illustrated in figure 3.1.

55. Toates (1979), cited after Siegel, Krank, and Hinson (1988), p. 85.

56. The following draws on O'Brien et al. (1992).

57. O'Brien et al. (1992), p. 404.

58. Eikelboom and Stewart (1982, 1997), Ramsay and Woods (1977).

59. O'Brien et al. (1992), p. 405.

60. Robinson (1993), pp. 374, 370.

61. Robinson (1993), pp. 387–388.

62. Gardner (1997).

63. Blum et al. (1996).

64. Gardner (1997), p. 67; references deleted.

Chapter 4

1. See Elster (1998d) for details.

2. Weber (1968), p. 30.

3. See, for instance, Coleman (1990), chaps. 10–11.

4. Elster (1989a, 1989b, 1990).

5. Here my terminology differs from that of Coleman (1990, p. 247), from whom I take this example.

6. The argument developed here involves three phenomena: social norms, moral values, and subjective preferences or "tastes." The common feature of the latter two, by virtue of which I have grouped them together, is that they do not rely on the approval or disapproval of other people. For other purposes, it may be useful to group the first two together, since the violation of both norms and moral values is capable of triggering strong emotions in the subject and in observers. For still other purposes, it may be useful to group the first and the third together, to the extent that both regulate purely personal choices that impose no externalities on others. As these comments show, these distinctions and classifications are purely heuristic and do not claim to have any intrinsic interest.

7. According to Kreps (1990a, 1990b), a major aspect of culture is to allow people to converge on one coordination equilibrium rather than another, by providing the appropriate beliefs.

8. The following draws on Egret (1950).

9. See Elster (1998c).

10. Thomas (1973), p. 108.

11. Taylor (1971).

12. Kuran (1995). For some critical comments, see Elster (1996).

13. Tocqueville (1955), p. 155 (translation modified). In *Democracy in America*, he similarly explains why it is so "difficult to be sure

that [the majority's opinion] has changed." It may happen that "the majority no longer believes, but it looks as if it did believe, and this empty ghost of public opinion is enough to chill the innovators and make them maintain their silent respect" (de Tocqueville 1969, p. 644).

14. For Marx, see Elster (1985), pp. 506–510; for Tocqueville, see Elster (1994), pp. 112–118.

15. Axelrod (1986), Abreu (1988), Akerlof (1976, 1980), Coleman (1990).

16. Elster (1989a), pp. 132–133.

17. Lovejoy (1961), pp. 181, 191, 199.

18. Wilson (1988), p. 203.

19. Busquet (1920), pp. 357–358. For a subtle discussion of the predicament of the man who fails to avenge an offense, see also Bourdieu (1969).

20. In this work I do not address the phenomena of self-deceptive beliefs and self-deceptive unawareness. I firmly believe that they exist, but I cannot answer the transcendental question of how they are possible. For recent discussions, see Mele (1997) and the accompanying comments, notably those of Bach (1997) and Sackeim and Gur (1997).

21. Lewis (1992), pp. 15–16.

22. Lewis (1992), p. 17. Compare Maxmen and Ward (1995), pp. 51–52: "Patients with major depression usually feel sad, yet some don't feel sad at all, but complain primarily of bodily aches and pains."

23. Levy (1973), p. 324; see also Levy (1984).

24. Williams (1993), Spacks (1995), Lewis (1936).

25. Williams (1993), p. 91; Spacks (1995), pp. 12–13.

26. Hochschild (1979), p. 567. What she actually writes is "One mother, a feminist, may feel that she should not feel as guilty as she does. The second, a traditionalist, may feel that she should feel more guilty than, in fact, she does feel." The suggestion that the feminist mother might feel shame and the traditionalist guilt is mine.

27. I assume that people may feel shame for emotions even when they do not believe there are tell-tale signs that will betray them to others. This assumption seems quite plausible, for instance, in the case of the feminist mother.

28. Ekman (1992b).

29. Note the difference between a belief triggering an emotional disposition and resulting in an emotion, and a belief *about* a disposition triggering an emotion.

30. Lewis (1992), p. 77; Tangney (1990), p. 103. The mere feeling of inferiority involved in envy, even without any shame attached, is also intensely unpleasant. The motivational power of envy is often double-barreled, involving both the first-order pain of inferiority and the second-order pain of shame.

31. Dover (1994), p. 70.

32. Dover (1994), p. 70.

33. Ober (1989), p. 276.

34. Miller claims that in modern societies "we learn to suffer *guilt* from mocking" (1997, p. 200; my italics). This is certainly often the case. When Emma Woodhouse makes fun of poor Miss Bates and receives a scolding from Mr. Knightley, what she feels is definitely guilt rather than shame, as shown by her efforts to make repairs. In other cases, though, what keeps people from mocking are social rather than moral norms, as shown by the fact that what counts as banter in some circles would be seen as mockery in others.

35. I thus disagree with Ben-Ze'ev (1992), who characterizes this emotion as envy.

36. Again I disagree with Ben-Ze'ev (1992), who treats physical disability and laziness on a par as cognitive conditions for (what he calls) envy.

37. Zinberg (1984), p. 27.

38. Orford (1985), p. 156; Zhang (1995), p. 49; Hanson (1995), p. 311; Hall (1986), p. 168.

39. Hanson (1995), p. 311.

40. Goodwin and Gabrielli (1997), p. 143.

41. Moene (1998).

42. With regard to cue-dependent craving, however, recommendations diverge. As I note in section 5.3 below, addicts trying to quit can adopt either the strategy of cue extinction or that of cue avoidance. According to Vaillant, Alcoholics Anonymous adopts the first strategy: "One reason abstinence for opiates under parole supervision and abstinence from alcohol under AA supervision are more enduring than abstinence achieved during hospitalization or imprisonment is that the former experiences occur in the community. Thus, abstinence is achieved in the presence of many conditioned reinforcers (community bars, other addicts, community hassles, and so on). For example, AA encourages the alcohol abuser to maintain a busy schedule of social activities and the serving of beverages (coffee) in the presence of former drinkers. Many of the secondary reinforcers are present. Only alcohol is missing. Such 'secondary reinforcers' lose their potency in controlling an addict's behavior most rapidly when such events occur in the absence of reinforcement" (1995, pp. 251–252). By contrast, Baumeister, Heatherton and Tice assert that the fact "that cues influence the desire to drink has not been lost on AA. Their meetings are held in churches or schools, which are places not previously associated with drinking" (1994, p. 162).

43. Glantz et al. (1996), p. 258.

44. The following draws heavily on the essays in Heath (1995b). Unless otherwise indicated, references below to national norms are drawn from the chapters on different countries in this volume.

45. Sidorov (1995), p. 247. With respect to opiate use, Zinberg similarly observes, "The experience of addiction diminishes personality differences and makes all compulsive users seem very much alike" (1984, p. 211). According to Gardner and David, "At the very outset and at late stages of recovery from drug addiction, humans are perhaps less similar to laboratory animals. But during the active addictive phase, and during both the acute and short-term withdrawal and abstinence phases, we are perhaps most similar to laboratory animals" (1998). Thus advanced addiction seems to obliterate or reduce cultural differences, personality differences, and differences between humans and nonhuman animals.

46. For a general discussion on the attitude of the world religions towards alcoholism, see Sournia (1986), pp. 184–200.

47. Mäkelä (1986), p. 26.

48. Heath (1995a), p. 334.

49. Moskalewicz and Zielinski (1995), p. 230.

50. MacAndrew and Edgerton (1969), p. 89–90; see also Edgerton (1985), pp. 61–69.

51. Gamella (1995), p. 365.

52. Nahoum-Grappe (1995), p. 80.

53. Moskalewicz and Zielinski (1995), p. 228.

54. Nyberg and Allebeck (1995), p. 286–287.

55. Heath (1995a), p. 344; see also p. 339.

56. Zhang (1995), p. 41.

57. Gamella (1995), p. 261.

58. Weiss (1995), p. 150; my italics.

59. Moskalewicz and Zielinski (1995), p. 232; my italics.

60. Samarasinghe (1995), p. 275.

61. Brehm (1966). The mechanism of reactance may also explain why some individuals block their desire for a good because they are told to consume it. Zinberg, for instance, reports, "The popularity of marihuana can act as a deterrent to beginning use for those of an independent spirit who automatically on personality grounds resist becoming passive followers" (1984, p. 85).

62. See the skeptical comments by June Tangney cited in "Crime and Punishment: Shame Gains Popularity as an Alternative to Prison," *New York Times*, January 16, 1997. For a general discussion of the relation between shame, shaming, and anger, see also Lewis (1992), pp. 149–153.

63. Orford (1985), p. 138.

64. Polivy and Herman (1993), p. 180; Heatherton and Baumeister (1991). Maxmen and Ward report that bulimics "continue to binge in order to delay the inevitable postbinge dysphoria" (1995, p. 343), which in 87 percent of the cases takes the form of guilt.

65. Baumeister, Heatherton, and Tice (1994), p. 227.

66. Rosenthal and Rugle (1994), p. 33–34.

67. Lichtenstein and Brown (1980), p. 194.

68. Moskalewicz and Zielinski (1995), p. 228.

69. Nahoum-Grappe (1995), p. 82

70. Mäkelä (1986), p. 21.

71. Oshodin (1995), p. 213.

72. Cottino (1995), p. 157.

73. Plant (1995), p. 290.

74. Rey (1995), p. 184.

75. Sidorov (1995), p. 244.

76. Oshodin (1995), p. 218.

77. Nahoum-Grappe (1995), p. 83.

78. Nahoum-Grappe (1995), p. 80.

79. Sournia (1986), pp. 104–106.

80. Sournia (1986), p. 106.

81. Zinberg (1984), p. 154.

82. Cited after Orford 1985, p. 73.

83. MacAndrew and Edgerton (1969), chaps. 1 and 2 respectively. Although recent findings show that they underestimated the disinhibiting effects of alcohol (Steele and Josephs 1990), this does not undermine their general argument.

84. Sournia (1986), p. 20.

85. Goldstein (1994), p. 106–107.

86. Orford (1985), p. 243–244.

87. Eiser, Sutton and Wober (1978), pp. 100, 106.

88. Levine (1978); Sournia (1986), p. 57; Brennan (1991); Nahoum-Grappe (1995), p. 80.

89. Levine (1978), p. 152.

90. Levine (1978), p. 154, n. 12.

91. The ability of alcoholics to return to moderate or controlled drinking remains controversial. Vaillant asserts as his conclusion, "Not that alcohol-dependent individuals never return to social drinking but only that it is a rare and often an unstable state" (1995, p. 297). A case in which an *unambiguously* false belief can prevent relapse is provided by subcutaneously implanted disulfiram (see section 5.3 below).

92. Babor et al. (1986), pp. 99, 107; my italics.

93. Steele and Josephs (1990).

94. Ashton and Stepney (1982).

Chapter 5

1. Watson (1998).

2. Watson (1998).

3. Watson (1998).

4. Watson (1998).

5. Davidson (1980), chap. 2.

6. In these stylized illustrations I ignore the fact that similar assumptions and inferences are needed to establish (provisionally) that the agent possesses the relevant bits of information. We might know that he read the article in which certain facts are reported, but not whether he remembers it correctly.

7. To illustrate, in order to form a belief about the relative value of two options, the agent has to add up the values of their components parts. Suppose that the correct sums are 39 and 40 and that he chooses the first option. To minimize his irrationality, we should assume that he made a slight mistake in arithmetic rather than assuming that he deliberately chose the inferior option.

8. In Elster (1998d) I argue that Max Weber's theory of action is flawed by a confusion of subjective *rationality* with objective *success*.

9. On this issue, see Winter (1964) and Elster (1984), chap. 2, sec. 4.

10. Hume (1960), p. 415.

11. Veyne (1976).

12. Elster (1997).

13. In a more tentative spirit, we can apply a similar argument to self-interested motivations. Although many persons give more weight to their own gratifications than to those of others, one might argue that the mere fact that these are *their* gratifications does not amount to a reason, although it may be associated with such reasons. If we disregard such facts as that we may be more efficient at promoting our own good than that of others and that an impersonal attitude may detract from the motivation to do anything at all, the welfare of any person is as valuable as that of any other. Yet this (putative) lack of reasons for treating other people differently does not detract from the explanatory power of self-interest.

14. See Loewenstein (1992) for a survey.

15. Mackie (1996), p. 1009; italics added.

16. Sartre (1936), Schafer (1976).

17. Solomon (1993), p. 222.

18. Solomon defines as guilt what I have defined as shame, and vice versa. The reference in the text uses my terminology.

19. Elster (1999).

20. Solomon (1993), p. 222.

21. Hochschild (1983), p. 25.

22. Hochschild (1983), p. 41.

23. On this feedback process, see Hatfield, Cacioppo, and Rapson (1994).

24. Montaigne (1991), p. 944.

25. Dawes (1994).

26. The contrast is from LeDoux (1996), p. 176.

27. Frijda (1986), pp. 80–81.

28. Montaigne (1991), p. 816. In a footnote to his translation M. A. Screech cites *Nicomachean Ethics* 1167b as the source for what Aristotle says. The correct reference is to 1116b.

29. Frijda (1986), p. 118.

30. *Nicomachean Ethics* 1312b, 19–34.

31. For somewhat skeptical comments on the effect of arousal, see Frijda (1986), pp. 112–115, and Isen (1993), p. 266.

32. See Isen (1993) for a survey.

33. See, notably, De Sousa (1987) and Damasio (1994).

34. Elster (1998a).

35. This is, for instance, the procedure adopted in Frank (1988) and Becker (1976).

36. Elster (1997).

37. Tesser and Achee (1994).

38. Technically, the dependent value has to be continuous rather than the dichotomous choice between stealing the book and not stealing or returning it. We can assume, therefore, that the dependent variable is a propensity to steal the book and that the agent proceeds to steal it once the propensity reaches a certain level.

39. Festinger (1957); see also Wicklund and Brehm (1976).

40. Tesser and Achee (1994), p. 104.

41. Festinger and Bramel (1962), p. 271.

42. Boyer (1996).

43. This corresponds to the argument in Loewenstein (1996, 1998) to the effect that visceral feelings such as shame undermine our ability to correctly imagine future subjective states.

44. Cited after Levine (1978), p. 152.

45. Heyman (1998), citing Cohen et al. (1971) and Bigelow and Liebson (1972).

46. Gawin (1991), p. 1581; my italics.

47. Gardner and David (1998).

48. Edwards et al. (1994), p. 119.

49. Orford (1985), p. 59; Uri and Boyd (1996), p. 12.

50. Edwards et al. (1994), p. 118.

51. Davidson (1980); see also Gjelsvik (1998).

52. See notably Ainslie (1992) for extensive discussions of this idea.

53. *Nicomachean Ethics* 1147a.

54. "The driver goes to a party and he judges it best to stop at two drinks in spite of the pleasure to be had from more, because there is nobody else to take the wheel on the way home. Nevertheless, when he is offered a third drink, which, we may suppose, is a double, he takes it. How can he? Easily, if the wish for a third drink biases his deliberation at the party before he takes it. For example, he might tell himself, against the weight of the evidence, that it is not dangerous to drive home after six measures of whiskey, or he might forget, under the influence of his wish, how many drinks he has already taken" (Pears 1985, p. 12).

55. Dawes (1988) and Baron (1995) are good surveys.

56. Viscusi (1992), p. 123.

57. Akerlof and Dickens (1982).

58. McKenna (1990).

59. In a study finding that coffee drinkers were less inclined to believe evidence of negative effects of caffeine, Kunda (1987, pp. 642–644) was able to eliminate the self-selection hypothesis by telling both male and female coffee drinkers that the risk arose in the context of breast cancer. Heavy female drinkers were less convinced by the evidence than low female drinkers, whereas no such difference was found in the male subjects. Agostinelli and Miller (1994) found that both abstainers and heavy drinkers exaggerate the *prevalence* of drinking in the population, the former (they argue) out of self-enhancement and the latter out of self-protection. The same motives induce abstainers to overestimate and drinkers to underestimate the negative *consequences* of drinking.

60. Wagenaar (1988), p. 13. See also Tversky and Kahneman (1974).

61. Wagenaar (1988), p. 109.

62. Dickerson (1984), p. 52.

63. Dickerson (1984), p. 134.

64. A gambler might exploit this mechanism to make money by selling "inside information." He might, for instance, "tell nine different people about the inside information on nine different horses. In this way he would have at least one, and possibly two or three people come to him the next time he touted. He would have more than one person because the people who received the second and

third horse that came in would think that the tout was close and 'if only' they had put the money to place or show it would have paid off" (Lesieur 1984, p. 180).

65. Gilovich (1983), p. 1122.

66. Cornish (1978), p. 108.

67. Becker (1996), p. 120. For a formal model of this phenomenon, see O'Donoghue and Rabin (1998).

68. Herrnstein and Prelec (1992), Becker and Murphy (1988), Orphanides and Zervos (1995).

69. Internalities are explained within the general framework of Herrnstein's "matching law" (see the articles collected in Herrnstein 1997). The matching law is also the basis for Ainslie's theory of hyperbolic discounting. Yet when Herrnstein and Prelec (1992) try to explain why addicts have difficulties quitting once they are hooked, they refer not to preference reversal but to withdrawal.

70. For a related argument, see Parducci (1995). In Parducci's model, the internality is due to a contrast effect rather than to a habituation effect.

71. Eliot Gardner (personal communication).

72. One might respond—in Chicago-style philosophy of economics—that models are to be tested only by their implications, not also by the realism of their assumptions. Even if we accept this (to me) dubious idea, Orphanides and Zervos do not in fact offer aggregate evidence for their theory.

73. In this context, let me mention an important "ignorance is bliss" result found by Juan Carillo and Thomas Mariotti (1997). They show that in some cases problems created by hyperbolic discounting may be overcome by "strategic ignorance." Specifically, they argue, "There is a tradeoff in the decision to acquire information. On the one hand, under full information, the agent can take the optimal action at the present date. On the other hand, due to perfect recall, this information is shared with all future incarnations." Because the agent can predict that the latter incarnations will be excessively present-oriented from his current point of view, he may not want them to be too well informed. Suppose, for instance, that the agent is afraid of HIV transmission through unprotected sex. Although he does not know how likely it is that the virus will be transmitted by a single act of intercourse, he has an initial subjective probability

distribution over this outcome. Given these priors, his optimal action is to abstain from unprotected sex. Yet he also has the (costless) option of finding out more, by asking a doctor or consulting statistical tables. He might then rationally decide to abstain from gathering that information if it might have the effect of lowering the estimate of transmission and induce a future incarnation to engage in unprotected sex because that will be optimal *from the point of view of that incarnation*. Applied to addiction, however, this line of argument would show that rational individuals may abstain from gathering information to *avoid* getting addicted.

74. Loewenstein (1996, 1998).

75. Fischhoff (1992), p. 137.

76. Gardner and David (1998). The heightened vulnerability referred to under (1) has been demonstrated in rats, where chronic exposure to heroin or cocaine produces irreversible changes in the reward neurons, which leads to "more of a euphorigenic effect than [in] other rats from the same dose of a given addictive drug" (Gardner and David 1998).

77. Elster (1984), chap. 2.

78. Ainslie (1992).

79. See Elster (1989a), pp. 201–202, and Bratman (1995) for claims that the belief in the causal efficacy of precedent is a form of magical thinking. In a reply to criticisms, Ainslie (1994) maintains that the belief is straightforwardly rational.

80. Skog (1998).

81. In O'Donoghue and Rabin (1998), the implications of this argument for addiction are spelled out in greater detail.

82. Helge Waal (personal communication). Strictly speaking, this fatalistic attitude does not amount to sophisticated choice as defined above. The addicts' prediction about what they will do is based not on an anticipation of what it will be rational for them to do in the last period of their planning horizon but on the idea that since most addicts seem to relapse, they too are likely to do so.

83. I discuss precommitment strategies more fully in Elster (1999). Since chap. 1, sec. 7, of that work deals extensively with precommitment and addiction, my discussion here has been kept to a minimum.

84. Cited after Orford (1985), p. 19; my italics.

85. Schelling (1992), p. 167.

86. Brown and Fromm (1987), chap. 4.

87. Miller and Hester (1980), pp. 31–42; Lichtenstein and Brown (1980), pp. 189–192.

88. Weiss, Mirin, and Bartel (1994), p. 149; Callahan (1980), pp. 158–159; Miller and Hester (1980), pp. 90–91; Miller (1980), pp. 276–277.

Chapter 6

1. Orford (1985), p. 195.

2. This is also true of the more purely visceral urge to urinate, which may subside when there is no conventionally accepted way of relieving it and then intensify very rapidly when the agent knows that there will soon be an occasion to do so.

3. Goldstein (1994), pp. 220–221.

4. LeDoux (1996), pp. 203, 243.

5. Watson (1998).

6. LeDoux (1996), p. 175.

7. *On Anger*, I.xviii.

8. Mittleman et al. (1995).

9. Kawachi et al. (1996).

10. Frijda (1986), p. 129.

11. See Barraclough (1994), pp. 94–100, and Dubovsky (1997), pp. 333–337, for surveys of the literature.

References

Abreu, D. (1988). "On the theory of infinitely repeated games with discounting." *Econometrica* 56: 383–396.

Agostinelli, G., and Miller, W. R. (1994). "Drinking and thinking: how does personal drinking affect judgments of prevalence and risk?" *Journal of Studies on Alcohol* 55: 327–337.

Ainslie, G. (1992). *Picoeconomics*. Cambridge: Cambridge University Press.

Ainslie, G. (1994). "Is rationality just a bookkeeping system?" Paper read at the American Philosophical Association, Los Angeles, 2 April 1994.

Akerlof, G. A. (1976). "The economics of caste and of the rat race and other woeful tales." *Quarterly Journal of Economics* 90: 599–617.

Akerlof, G. A. (1980). "A theory of social custom, of which unemployment may be one consequence." *Quarterly Journal of Economics* 94: 749–775.

Akerlof, G. A., and Dickens, W. (1982). "The economic consequences of cognitive dissonance." *American Economic Review* 72: 307–319.

Altman, J., et al. (1996). "The biological, social, and clinical bases of drug addiction." *Psychopharmacology* 125: 285–345.

American Psychiatric Association (1994). *Diagnostic and Statistical Manual of Mental Disorders*. Fourth ed. Washington, D. C.

Ashton, H., and Stepney, R. (1982). *Smoking*. London: Tavistock.

Axelrod, R. (1986). "An evolutionary approach to norms." *American Political Science Review* 80: 1095–1111.

Babcock, L., et al. (1995). "Biased judgments of fairness in bargaining." *American Economic Review* 85: 1337–1343.

Babcock, L., and Loewenstein, G. (1997). "Explaining bargaining impasse: the role of self-serving biases." *Journal of Economic Perspectives* 11: 109–126.

Babor, T. F., et al. (1986). "Concepts of alcoholism among American, French-Canadian, and French alcoholics." In T. F. Babor (ed.), *Alcohol and Culture: Comparative Perspectives from Europe and America*, pp. 98–109. New York: New York Academy of Sciences.

Bach, K. (1997). "Thinking and believing in self-deception." Comment on Mele 1997. *Behavioral and Brain Sciences* 20: 105.

Banaji, M. R., and Steele, C. M. (1989). "The social cognition of alcohol use." *Social Cognition* 7: 137–151.

Baron, J. (1995). *Thinking and Deciding*. Cambridge: Cambridge University Press.

Barraclough, J. (1994). *Cancer and Emotion*. New York: Wiley.

Baumeister, R. F., Heatherton, T. F., and Tice, D. M. (1994). *Losing Control: How and Why People Fail at Self-Regulation*. San Diego: Academic Press.

Becker, G. (1976). *The Economic Approach to Human Behavior*. Chicago: University of Chicago Press.

Becker, G. (1996). *Accounting for Tastes*. Cambridge: Harvard University Press.

Becker, G., and Murphy, K. (1988). "A theory of rational addiction." *Journal of Political Economy* 96: 675–700.

Ben-Ze'ev, A. (1992). "Envy and inequality." *Journal of Philosophy* 89: 551–581.

Bigelow, B., and Liebson, I. (1972). "Cost factors controlling alcoholic drinking." *Psychological Record* 22: 305–314.

Blum, K., et al. (1996). "Reward deficiency syndrome." *American Scientist* 84: 132–245.

Bourdieu, P. (1969). "The sentiment of honour in Kabyle society." In J. G. Peristiany (ed.), *Honour and Shame: The Values of Mediterranean Society*, pp. 191–241. Chicago: University of Chicago Press.

Bourgois, P. (1995). *In Search of Respect*. Cambridge: Cambridge University Press.

Boyer, P. (1996). "Admiral Boorda's war." *New Yorker*, 16 September.

Bozarth, R. (1990). "Drug addiction as a psychobiological process." In D. M. Warburton (ed.), *Addiction Controversies*, pp. 112–134. Chur, Switzerland: Harvood.

Bratman, M. (1995). "Planning and temptation." In L. May, M. Friedman, and A. Clark (eds.), *Mind and Morals*, pp. 293–310. Cambridge: MIT Press.

Brehm, J. (1966). *A Theory of Psychological Reactance*. New York: Academic Press.

Brennan, T. (1991). "Social drinking in old regime Paris." In S. Barrows and R. Room (eds.), *Drinking: Behavior and Belief in Modern History*, pp. 61–86. Berkeley: University of California Press.

Brothers, L. (1995). "Neurophysiology of the perception of intentions by primates." In M. Gazzaniga (ed.), *The Cognitive Neurosciences*, pp. 1107–1116. Cambridge: MIT Press.

Brown, D. P., and Fromm, E. (1987). *Hypnosis and Behavioral Medicine*. Hillsdale, N.J.: Lawrence Erlbaum.

Budd, M. (1995). *Values of Art*. London: Allen Lane.

Busquet, J. (1920). *Le droit de vendetta et les paci corses*. Paris: Pedone.

Callahan, E. J. (1980). "Alternative strategies in the treatment of narcotic addiction: a review." In W. R. Miller (ed.), *The Addictive Behaviors*, pp. 143–168. Oxford: Pergamon Press.

Cameron, L. (1995). "Raising the stakes in the ultimatum game: experimental evidence from Indonesia." Working paper no. 345, Industrial Relations Section, Princeton University.

Carillo, J., and Mariotti, T. (1997). "Wishful thinking and strategic ignorance." Unpublished manuscript, ECARE, Université Libre de Bruxelles, and GEMAQ, Université de Toulouse.

Carroll, N. (1996). *Theorizing the Moving Image*. Cambridge: Cambridge University Press.

Childress, A. R., et al. (1992). "Classically conditioned factors in drug dependence." In J. H. Lowinson et al. (eds.), *Substance Abuse: A Comprehensive Handbook*, 2nd ed., pp. 56–69. Baltimore: Williams and Wilkins.

Cohen, M., et al. (1971). "Alcoholism: controlled drinking and incentives for abstinence." *Psychological Reports* 28: 575–580.

Coleman, J. (1990). *Foundations of Social Theory*. Cambridge: Harvard University Press.

Cornish, D. B. (1978). *Gambling: A Review of the Literature and Its Implications for Policy and Research*. London: Her Majesty's Stationery Office.

Cottino, A. (1995). "Italy." In Heath (1995b), pp. 156–167.

Damasio, A. (1994). *Descartes' Error*. New York: Putnam.

Davidson, D. (1980). *Essays on Actions and Events*. Oxford: Oxford University Press.

Dawes, R. (1988). *Rational Choice in an Uncertain World*. Fort Worth: Harcourt Brace Jovanovich.

Dawes, R. (1994). *House of Cards*. New York: Free Press.

De Sousa, R. (1987). *The Rationality of Emotion*. Cambridge: MIT Press.

De Waal, F. (1996). *Good Natured*. Cambridge: Harvard University Press.

Dickerson, M. G. (1984). *Compulsive Gamblers*. London: Longman.

Djilas, M. (1958). *Land without Justice*. London: Methuen.

Dover, K. (1994). *Greek Popular Morality*. Indianapolis: Hackett.

Doweiko, H. (1996). *Concepts of Chemical Dependency*. Pacific Grove: Brooks/Cole.

Dubovsky, S. L. (1997). *Mind-Body Deceptions*. New York: Norton.

Edgerton, R. (1985). *Rules, Exceptions, and the Social Order*. Berkeley: University of California Press.

Edwards, G., et al. (1994). *Alcohol Policy and the Public Good*. Oxford: Oxford University Press.

Egret, J. (1950). *La révolution des notables*. Paris: Armand Colin.

Eikelboom, R., and Stewart, J. (1982). "Conditioning of drug-induced physiological response." *Psychological Review* 89: 507–528.

Eiser, J., Sutton, S., and Wober, M. (1978). " 'Consonant' and 'dissonant' smokers and the self-attribution of addiction." *Addictive Behaviors* 3: 99–106.

Ekman, P. (1992a). "An argument for basic emotions." *Cognition and Emotion* 6: 169–200.

Ekman, P. (1992b). *Telling Lies*. New York: Norton.

Elster, J. (1983). *Sour Grapes*. Cambridge: Cambridge University Press.

Elster, J. (1984). *Ulysses and the Sirens*. Cambridge: Cambridge University Press.

Elster, J. (1985). *Making Sense of Marx*. Cambridge: Cambridge University Press.

Elster J. (1989a). *The Cement of Society: A Study of Social Order*. Cambridge: Cambridge University Press.

Elster, J. (1989b). "Social norms and economic theory." *Journal of Economic Perspectives* 31: 99–118.

Elster, J. (1990). "Norms of revenge." *Ethics* 100: 862–885.

Elster, J. (1993). *Political Psychology*. Cambridge: Cambridge University Press.

Elster, J. (1994). "The psychology of *Democracy in America*." In *The Great Ideas Today*. Chicago: Encyclopedia Britannica.

Elster, J. (1996). Review of Kuran (1995). *Acta Sociologica* 39: 113–115.

Elster, J. (1997). Review of Becker (1996). *University of Chicago Law Review* 64: 749–764.

Elster, J. (1998a). "Emotions and economic theory." *Journal of Economic Literature* 36: 47–74.

Elster, J. (1998b). "Gambling and addiction." In J. Elster and O.-J. Skog (eds.), *Getting Hooked: Rationality and the Addictions*. Cambridge: Cambridge University Press.

Elster, J. (1998c). "Accountability in Athenian politics." In B. Manin, A. Przeworski, and S. Stokes (eds.), *Democracy, Accountability, and Representation*. Cambridge: Cambridge University Press.

Elster J. (1998d). "Rationality, economy, and society." In S. Turner (ed.), *The Cambridge Companion to Weber*. Cambridge: Cambridge University Press.

Elster, J. (1998e). *Alchemies of the Mind*. Cambridge: Cambridge University Press.

Elster, J. (1998f). "Coming to terms with the past." *Archives Européennes de Sociologie* 39: 7–48.

Elster, J. (1999). *Ulysses Unbound*. Cambridge: Cambridge University Press.

Elster, J., and Loewenstein, G. (1992). "Utility from memory and anticipation." In G. Loewenstein and J. Elster (eds.), *Choice over Time*, pp. 213–234. New York: Russell Sage Foundation.

Festinger, L. (1957). *A Theory of Cognitive Dissonance*. Stanford: Stanford University Press.

Festinger, L., and Bramel, D. (1962). "The reactions of humans to cognitive dissonance." In A. Bachrach (ed.), *The Experimental Foundations of Clinical Psychology*, pp. 254–279. New York: Basic Books.

Fischhoff, B. (1992). "Risk taking: a developmental approach." In J. F. Yates (ed.), *Risk-Taking Behavior*, pp. 133–162. New York: Wiley.

Frank, R. (1988). *Passions within Reason*. New York: Norton.

Frijda, N. (1986). *The Emotions*. Cambridge: Cambridge University Press.

Fry, R. (1921). *Vision and Design*. New York: Brentano.

Gamella, J. F. (1995). "Spain." In Heath (1995b), pp. 254–269.

Gardner, E. (1997). "Brain reward mechanisms." In J. H. Lowinson et al. (eds.), *Substance Abuse: A Comprehensive Handbook*, 3rd ed., pp. 51–85. Baltimore: Williams Wilkins.

Gardner, E., and David, J. (1998). "The neurobiology of chemical addiction." In J. Elster and O.-J. Skog (eds.), *Getting Hooked: Rationality and the Addictions*. Cambridge: Cambridge University Press.

Gawin, F. (1991). "Cocaine addiction: psychology and neurophysiology." *Science* 251: 1580–1586.

Gilovich, T. (1983). "Biased evaluation and persistence on gambling." *Journal of Personality and Social Psychology* 44: 1110–1126.

Gjelsvik, O. (1998). "Addiction, weakness of will, and relapse." In J. Elster and O.-J. Skog (eds.), *Getting Hooked: Rationality and the Addictions*. Cambridge: Cambridge University Press.

Glantz, S., et al. (1986). *The Cigarette Papers*. Berkeley: University of California Press.

Gloor, P. (1986). "The role of the human limbic system in perception, memory, and affect." In J. P. Aggleton (ed.), *The Amygdala*. New York: Wiley, 1992.

Goldstein, A. (1994). *Addiction*. New York: Freeman.

Goodwin, D. W., and Gabrielli, W. F. (1997). "Alcohol: Clinical aspects." In J. H. Lowinson et al. (eds.), *Substance Abuse: A Comprehensive Textbook*, 3rd ed., pp. 142–148. Baltimore: Williams Wilkins.

Gordon, R. M. (1987). *The Structure of Emotions*. Cambridge: Cambridge University Press.

Gossop, M. (1990). "Compulsion craving and conflict." In D. M. Warburton (ed.), *Addiction Controversies*, pp. 236–249. Chur, Switzerland: Harvood.

Gray, J. A. (1991). *The Psychology of Fear and Stress*. Cambridge: Cambridge University Press.

Hall, R. L. (1986). "Alcohol treatment in American Indian populations." In T. F. Babor (ed.), *Alcohol and Culture: Comparative Perspectives from Europe and America*, pp. 168–178. New York: New York Academy of Sciences.

Hanson, D. J. (1995). "The United States of America." In Heath (1995b), pp. 300–315.

Hatfield, E., Cacioppo, J., and Rapson, R. (1994). *Emotional Contagion*. Cambridge: Cambridge University Press.

Heath, D. B. (1995a). "An anthropological view of alcohol and culture in international perspective." In Heath (1995b), pp. 328–347.

Heath, D. B., ed. (1995b). *International Handbook on Alcohol and Culture*. Westport, Conn.: Greenwood Press.

Heatherton, T. F., and Baumeister, R. F. (1991). "Binge eating as escape from self-awareness." *Psychological Bulletin* 110: 87–108.

Herrnstein, R. (1997). *The Matching Law*. Cambridge: Harvard University Press.

Herrnstein, R., and Prelec, D. (1992). "A theory of addiction." In G. Loewenstein and J. Elster (eds.), *Choice over Time*, pp. 331–360. New York: Russell Sage Foundation.

Heyman, G. (1998). "A scientific look at the idea that addiction is a chronic, relapsing disease." Working paper, Drugs and Addiction Group, Harvard University.

Hochschild, A. (1979). "Emotion work, feeling rules, and social structure." *American Journal of Sociology* 85: 551–575.

Hochschild, A. R. (1983). *The Managed Heart*. Berkeley: University of California Press.

Hoebel, B. G. (forthcoming). "Neural systems for reinforcement and inhibition of behavior: relevance to eating, addiction, and depression." In D. Kahneman, E. Diener, and N. Schwartz (eds.), *Understanding Quality of Life: Scientific Perspectives on Enjoyment and Suffering*. New York: Russell Sage.

Hume, D. (1960). *A Treatise of Human Nature*. Second edition. Edited by L. A. Selby-Bigge. Oxford: Oxford University Press.

Isen, A. (1993). "Positive affect and decision making." In Lewis and Haviland, (eds.), *Handbook of Emotions*, pp. 261–278. New York: Guilford Press.

Jellinek, E. M. (1960). *The Disease Concept of Alcoholism*. New Haven: Hillhouse Press.

Kawachi, I., et al. (1996). "A prospective study of anger and coronary heart disease." *Circulation* 94: 2090–2095.

Klein, R. (1993). *Cigarettes Are Sublime*. Durham: Duke University Press.

Kluger, R. (1996). *Ashes to Ashes*. New York: Knopf.

Kreps, D. (1990a). *Game Theory and Economic Modelling*. Oxford: Oxford University Press.

Kreps, D. (1990b). "Corporate culture and economic theory." In J. E. Alt and K. A. Shepsle (eds.), *Perspectives on Political Economy*, pp. 90–143. Cambridge: Cambridge University Press.

Krogh, D. (1991). *Smoking*. New York: Freeman.

Kunda, Z. (1987). "Motivated inference: self-serving generation and evaluation of causal theories." *Journal of Personality and Social Psychology* 53: 636–647.

Kuran, T. (1995). *Private Truths, Public Lies: The Social Consequences of Preference Falsification*. Cambridge: Harvard University Press.

Kurtz, E. (1979). *Not-God: A History of Alcoholics Anonymous*. Center City, Minnesota: Hazelden Educational Services.

LeDoux, J. (1993). "Emotional networks in the brain." In M. Lewis and J. M. Haviland (eds.), *Handbook of Emotions*, pp. 109–118. New York: Guilford Press.

LeDoux, J. (1995). "In search of an emotional system in the brain." In M. Gazzaniga (ed.), *The Cognitive Neurosciences*, pp. 1049–1061. Cambridge: MIT Press.

LeDoux, J. (1996). *The Emotional Brain*. New York: Simon and Schuster.

Lesieur, H. R. (1984). *The Chase: The Compulsive Gambler*. Rochester, Vermont: Schenkman Books.

Levenson, R. W. (1992). "Autonomic nervous system differences among emotions." *Psychological Science* 3: 23–27.

Levine, H. (1978). "The discovery of addiction." *Journal of Studies on Alcohol* 39: 143–174.

Levy, R. (1973). *The Tahitians*. Chicago: University of Chicago Press.

Levy, R. (1984). "Emotion, knowing, and culture." In R. A. Shweder and R. A. LeVine (eds.), *Culture Theory: Essays on Mind, Self, and Emotion*, pp. 214–237. Cambridge: Cambridge University Press.

Lewis, C. S. (1936). *The Allegory of Love*. Oxford: Oxford University Press.

Lewis, M. (1992). *Shame*. New York: Free Press.

Lichtenstein, E., and Brown, R. A. (1980). "Smoking cessation methods: review and recommendations." In W. R. Miller (ed.), *The Addictive Behaviors*, pp. 169–206. Oxford: Pergamon Press.

Liebowitz, M. (1983). *The Chemistry of Love*. Boston: Little, Brown.

Loewenstein, G. (1992). "The fall and rise of psychological explanations in the economics of intertemporal choice." In J. Elster and G. Loewenstein (eds.), *Choice over Time*, pp. 3–34. New York: Russell Sage Foundation.

Loewenstein, G. (1996). "Out of control: visceral influences on behavior." *Organizational Behavior and Human Decision Processes* 65: 272–292.

Loewenstein, G. (1998). "A visceral theory of addiction." In J. Elster and O.-J. Skog (eds.), *Getting Hooked: Rationality and the Addictions*. Cambridge: Cambridge University Press.

Loewenstein, G., et al. (1993). "Self-serving assessments of fairness and pretrial bargaining." *Journal of Legal Studies* 22: 135–159.

Loewenstein, G., and Schkade, D. (1998). "Wouldn't it be nice? Predicting future feelings." In D. Kahneman, E. Diener, and N. Schwartz (eds.), *Understanding Quality of Life: Scientific Perspectives on Enjoyment and Suffering*. New York: Russell Sage Foundation.

Lovejoy, A. O. (1961). *Reflections on Human Nature*. Baltimore: Johns Hopkins University Press.

MacAndrew, C., and Edgerton, R. (1969). *Drunken Comportment*. Chicago: Aldine.

Mackie, G. (1996). "Ending footbinding and infibulation: a convention account." *American Sociological Review* 61: 999–1017.

Mäkelä, K. (1986). "Attitudes towards drinking and drunkenness in four Scandinavian countries." In T. F. Babor (ed.), *Alcohol and*

Culture: Comparative Perspectives from Europe and America, pp. 21–32. New York: New York Academy of Sciences.

Margolin, A., and Avants, S. K. (1992). "Cue-reactivity and cocaine addiction." In T. R. Kosten and H. D. Kleber (eds.), *Clinician's Guide to Cocaine Addiction*, pp. 109–127. New York: Guilford Press.

Marks, I. (1987). *Fears, Phobias, and Rituals*. Oxford: Oxford University Press.

Marks, I. (1990). "Behavioural (non-chemical) addictions." *British Journal of Addiction* 85: 1389–1394.

Maxmen, J. S., and Ward, N. G. (1995). *Essential Psychopathology and Its Treatment*. New York: Norton.

McKenna, F. A. (1990)."Heuristics or cognitive deficits: how should we characterize smokers' decision making?" In D. M. Warburton (ed.), *Addiction Controversies*, pp. 261–270. Chur, Switzerland: Harvood.

McKim, W. (1991). *Drugs and Behavior*. Englewood Cliffs, N.J.: Prentice-Hall.

Mele, A. (1997). "Real self-deception." *Behavioral and Brain Sciences* 20: 91–102.

Miller, P. M. (1980). "Theoretical and practical issues in substance abuse assessment and treatment." In W. R. Miller (ed.), *The Addictive Behaviors*, pp. 265–290. Oxford: Pergamon Press.

Miller, W. I. (1997). *The Anatomy of Disgust*. Cambridge: Harvard University Press.

Miller, W. R., and Hester, R. K. (1980). "Treating the problem drinker: modern approaches." In W. R. Miller (ed.), *The Addictive Behaviors*, pp. 11–142. Oxford: Pergamon Press.

Mittleman, M. A., et al. (1995). "Triggering of acute myocardial infarction onset by episodes of anger." *Circulation* 92: 172–225.

Moene, K. O. (1998). "Addiction and social interaction." In J. Elster and O.-J. Skog (eds.), *Getting Hooked: Rationality and the Addictions*. Cambridge: Cambridge University Press.

Montaigne, M. de (1991). *The Complete Essays*. Translated by M. A. Screech. Harmondsworth: Penguin.

Moskalewicz, J., and Zielinski, A. (1995). "Poland." In Heath (1995b), pp. 224–236.

Nahoum-Grappe, V. (1995). "France." In Heath (1995b), pp. 75–87.

Nyberg, K., and Allebeck, P. (1995). "Sweden." In Heath (1995b), pp. 280–288.

Ober, J. (1989). *Mass and Elite in Democratic Athens*. Princeton: Princeton University Press.

O'Brien, C., et al. (1992). "Classical conditioning in drug-dependent humans." *Annals of New York Academy of Science* 54: 400–415.

O'Donogue, T., and Rabin, M. (1998). "Addiction and self-control." Unpublished manuscript.

Orford, J. (1985). *Excessive Appetites: A Psychological View of the Addictions*. Chichester: Wiley.

Orphanides, A., and Zervos, D. (1995). "Rational addiction with learning and regret." *Journal of Political Economy* 103: 739–758.

Oshodin, O. G. (1995). "Nigeria." In Heath (1995b), pp. 213–223.

Osiatynski, W. (1997). *Alcoholism: Sin or Disease?* Warsaw: Stefan Batory Foundation.

Panksepp, J. (1993). "Neurochemical controls of moods and emotions: amino acids and neuropeptides." In M. Lewis and J. M. Haviland (eds.), *Handbook of Emotions*, pp. 87–107. New York: Guilford Press.

Parducci, A. (1995). *Happiness, Pleasure, and Judgment*. Mahwah, N.J.: Lawrence Erlbaum.

Pascal, B. (1670). *Pensées*. Edited by P. Sellier. Paris: Bordas, 1991.

Pears, D. (1985). *Motivated Irrationality*. Oxford: Oxford University Press.

Peck, C. P. (1986). "Risk-taking behavior and compulsive gambling." *American Psychologist* 41: 461–465.

Peele, S. (1985). *The Meaning of Addiction*. Lexington, Mass.: Lexington Books.

Peele, S., and Brodsky, A. (1991). *Love and Addiction*. New York: Signet Books.

Plant, M. A. (1995). "The United Kingdom." In Heath (1995b), pp. 289–299.

Polivy, J., and Herman, C. P. (1993). "Etiology of binge eating: psychological mechanisms." In C. G. Fairburn and G. T. Wilson (eds.), *Binge Eating*, pp. 173–205. New York: Guilford Press.

Proust, M. (1954). *A la recherche du temps perdu*. Vols. 1–3. Ed. de la Pléiade. Paris: Gallimard.

Ramsay, D. S., and Woods, S. C. (1977). "Biological consequences of drug administration: implications for acute and chronic tolerance." *Psychological Review* 104: 170–193.

Rey, G. N. (1995). "Mexico." In Heath (1995b), pp. 179–189.

Robinson, T. E. (1993). "Persisting sensitizing effects of drugs on brain dopamine systems and behavior: implications for addiction and relapse." In S. G. Korenman and J. D. Barchas (eds.), *Biological Basis of Substance Abuse*, pp. 373–402. Oxford: Oxford University Press.

Robinson, T. E., and Berridge, K. C. (1993). "The neural basis of drug craving: an incentive-sensitization theory of addiction." *Brain Research Reviews* 18: 247–291.

Rosenthal, R. J., and Rugle, L. J. (1994). "A psychodynamic approach to the treatment of pathological gambling. Part I: Achieving abstinence." *Journal of Gambling Studies* 10: 21–42.

Roth, A. (1995). "Bargaining experiments." In J. H. Kagel and A. E. Roth (eds.), *Handbook of Experimental Economics*, pp. 253–348. Princeton: Princeton University Press.

Sackeim, H. A., and Gur, R. C. (1997). "Flavors of self-deception." Comment on Mele 1997. *Behavioral and Brain Research* 20: 125–126.

Samarasinghe, D. (1995). "Sri Lanka." In Heath (1995b), pp. 270–279.

Sartre, J.-P. (1936). *Esquisse d'une théorie des émotions*. Paris: Hermann.

Satel, S. (1992). " 'Craving for and fear of cocaine': a phenomenological update in cocaine craving and paranoia." In T. R. Kosten and H. D. Kleber (eds.), *Clinician's Guide to Cocaine Addiction*, pp. 172–192. New York: Guilford Press.

Schafer, R. (1976). *A New Language for Psychoanalysis*. New Haven: Yale University Press.

Schelling, T. C. (1992). "Self-control." In G. Loewenstein and J. Elster (eds.), *Choice over Time*, pp. 167–176. New York: Russell Sage Foundation.

Schelling, T. C. (1998). "Rationally coping with lapses from rationality." In J. Elster and O.-J. Skog (eds.), *Getting Hooked: Rationality and the Addictions*. Cambridge: Cambridge University Press.

Schmitz, J. M., Schneider, N. G., and Jarvik, M. E. (1997). "Nicotine." In J. H. Lowinson et al. (eds.), *Substance Abuse*, 3rd edition, pp. 276–294. Baltimore: Williams and Wilkins.

Schultz, W., Dayan, P., and Montague, P. R. (1997). "A neural substrate of prediction and reward." *Science* 275: 1593–1599.

Seeburger, F. (1993). *Addiction and Responsibility*. New York: Crossroad.

Sellier, P., ed. (1991). *Pascal: Pensées*. Paris: Bordas.

Servan-Schreiber, D., and Perlstein, W. M. (1997). "Selective limbic activation and its relevance to emotional disorders." Unpublished manuscript, School of Medicine, University of Pittsburgh.

Sidorov P. I. (1995). "Russia." In Heath (1995b), pp. 237–253.

Siegel, S., Krank, M. D., and Hinson, R. E. (1988). "Anticipation of pharmacological and nonpharmacological events: classical conditioning and addictive behavior." In Stanton Peele (ed.), *Visions of Addiction*, pp. 85–116. New York: Lexington Books.

Simon, E. (1997). "Opiates: neurobiology." In J. H. Lowinson et al. (eds.), *Substance Abuse*, 3rd edition, pp. 148–157. Baltimore: Williams and Wilkins.

Skog, O.-J. (1998). "Hyperbolic discounting, willpower, and addiction." Unpublished manuscript.

Solomon, R. C. (1993). *The Passions*. Indianapolis: Hackett.

Solomon, R. L., and Corbit, J. D. (1974). "An opponent-process theory of motivation." *Psychological Review* 81: 119–145.

Sournia, J.-C. (1986). *L'alcoolisme*. Paris: Flammarion.

Spacks, P. M. (1995). *Boredom*. University of Chicago Press.

Spealman, R. (1979). "Behavior maintained by termination of a schedule of self-administered cocaine." *Science* 204: 1231–1233.

Stall, R., and Biernacki, P. (1986). "Spontaneous remission from the problematic use of substances." *International Journal of Addictions* 21: 1–23.

Steele, C. M., and Josephs, R. A. (1990). "Alcohol myopia." *American Psychologist* 45: 921–933.

Stendhal (1980). *De l'amour*. Edited by V. Del Litto. Paris: Gallimard.

Tangney, J. P. (1990). "Assessing individual differences in proneness to shame and guilt: development of the self-conscious affect and attribution inventory." *Journal of Personality and Social Psychology* 59: 102–111.

Taylor, C. (1971). "Interpretation and the science of man." *Review of Metaphysics* 3: 25–51.

Tennov, D. (1979). *Love and Limerence*. New York: Stein and Day.

Tesser, A. (1991). "Emotion in social comparison processes." In J. Suls and T. A. Wills (eds.), *Social Comparison*, pp. 115–145. Hillsdale, N.J.: Lawrence Erlbaum.

Tesser, A., and Achee, J. (1994). "Aggression, love, conformity, and other social psychological catastrophes." In R. R. Vallacher and A. Nowak (eds.), *Dynamical Systems in Social Psychology*, pp. 96–109. New York: Academic Press.

Thomas, K. (1973). *Religion and the Decline of Magic*. Harmondsworth: Penguin Books.

Thompson, D'Arcy W. (1992). *On Growth and Form*. New York: Dover.

Toates, F. M. (1979). "Homeostasis and drinking behavior." *Behavioral and Brain Sciences* 2: 95–139.

Tocqueville, A. de (1955). *The Old Regime and the French Revolution*. New York: Anchor Books

Tocqueville, A. de (1969). *Democracy in America*. New York: Anchor Books.

Tversky, A., and Kahneman, D. (1974). "Judgment under uncertainty." *Science* 185: 1124–1130.

Twerski, A. (1990). *Addictive Thinking*. New York: Harper Collins.

Uri, N. D., and Boyd, R. (1996). "The effects of increasing the tobacco excise tax on the U.S. economy." *Journal of Health and Social Policy* 8: 1–23.

Vaillant, G. (1995). *The Natural History of Alcoholism Revisited*. Cambridge: Harvard University Press.

Veyne, P. (1976). *Le pain et le cirque*. Paris: Editions du Seuil.

Viscusi, K. (1992). *Smoking*. Oxford: Oxford University Press.

Vollmer, P. J. (1977). "Do mischievous dogs reveal their 'guilt'?" *Veterinary Medicine Small Animal Clinician* 72: 1002–1005.

Wagenaar, W. A. (1988). *Paradoxes of Gambling Behaviour*. Hove and London: Lawrence Erlbaum.

Walton, K. (1990). *Mimesis as Make-Believe*. Cambridge: Harvard University Press.

Warburton, D. (1990). "All substance use pleasures are not the same." In D. M. Warburton (ed.), *Addiction controversies*, pp. 45–52. Chur, Switzerland: Harvood.

Watson, G. (1998). "Disordered appetites." Unpublished manuscript.

Weber, M. (1968). *Economy and Society*. New York: Bedminster Press.

Weiss, R. D., Mirin, M. D., and Bartel, R. L. (1994). *Cocaine*. Washington: American Psychiatric Press.

Weiss, S. (1995). "Israel." In Heath (1995b), pp. 142–155.

Wickelgren, I. (1997). "Getting the brain's attention." *Science* 278: 35–37.

Wicklund, R. A., and Brehm, J. (1976). *Perspectives on Cognitive Dissonance*. Hillsdale, N.J.: Erlbaum.

Williams, B. A. O. (1993). *Shame and Necessity*. Berkeley: University of California Press.

Wilson, S. (1988). *Feuding, Conflict, and Banditry in Nineteenth-Century Corsica*. Cambridge: Cambridge University Press.

Winter, S. (1964). "Economic 'natural selection' and the theory of the firm." *Yale Economic Essays* 4: 225–272.

Yanal, R. J. (1994). "The paradox of emotion and fiction." *Pacific Philosophical Quarterly* 75: 54–75.

Zhang Jiacheng (1995). "China." In Heath (1995b), pp. 42–50.

Zinberg, N. (1984). *Drug, Set, and Setting: The Basis for Controlled Intoxicant Use*. New Haven: Yale University Press.

Index